GW01606815

NOTE

Carriage of this Code on board United Kingdom registered vessels is required by The Merchant Shipping (Code of Safe Working Practices) Regulations 1980, (Statutory Instrument 1980 No 686), which stipulates how many copies must be carried.

DEPARTMENT OF TRADE

Code of safe working practices for merchant seamen

LONDON
HER MAJESTY'S STATIONERY OFFICE

First published 1978
Third impression 1981

Cover illustration reproduced
by kind permission of the
General Council of British Shipping

ISBN 0 11 512031 9

Contents

CHAPTER 1

General

1 Introduction

1.1 This Code provides information and guidance on procedures to be followed and measures to be adopted for improving the safety and health of those living and working on board ship.

1.2 The Code is addressed to everyone on a ship regardless of rank or rating because the recommendations can be effective only if they are understood by all and if all cooperate in their implementation. Those not themselves actually engaged in a job in hand should be aware of what is being done, so that they may avoid putting themselves at risk or those concerned at risk by impeding or needlessly interfering with the conduct of the work.

1.3 The seafarer should always have regard for his own safety but also care for the safety of others.

1.4 Owners, managers and shore staff should at all times support those on board the ships for which they are responsible, by ensuring that equipment and supplies required for safety purposes are available to the ships. Where special hazards arise on installed ships' equipment or in the use of consumable stores, the necessary instructions or advice should be made available to the ships.

1.5 This Code may be supplemented by other codes, guides or instructions on safety that may be issued by companies to particular ships.

1.6 This Code is arranged so that matters which concern every seafarer on every ship are dealt with in the earlier Chapters, then follows advice on different sorts of jobs common to most ships and lastly come provisions related to work particular to special kinds of ship.

1.7 The aim has been to state what is accepted as normal, safe practice but ships differ in construction, layout and equipment, in function and in conditions of service. In the circumstances of an individual ship, it may be impracticable or inadvisable for some reason to comply exactly with a recommended practice. In such instances, the Code provisions will usually indicate the nature of the principal risks and care should be taken to adopt an alternative method which adequately guards against those risks and which does not itself introduce any special new hazard.

1.8 Not every contingency can be covered specifically in a Code of Practice but, in a situation which has not been covered, the experienced seafarer who is conversant with this Code should usually be able to identify in the new situation features of similarity to those in some other situation or operation which has been dealt with in the Code and apply in principle the safeguards mentioned therein.

1.9 Where a ship or an item of her equipment has novel features, consideration should be given to any hazards presented thereby which may require special precautions to be taken. Any information or working instructions provided should be carefully studied to that end.

1.10 Recommendations are necessarily framed in broad terms covering only aspects related to the particular operation described. It is the responsibility of those concerned in carrying out the operation to ensure that it is done in all other respects in a seamanlike fashion and safely even though details of every necessary precaution may not have been explicitly stated in the relevant provision of the Code.

1.11 Some provisions of this Code relate to matters which are the subject of statutory regulations. Such recommendations are intended to give guidance on how the statutory obligations should be fulfilled. In no case are the recommendations to be regarded as supplanting or amending the relevant legal requirements.

1.12 Accidents have often resulted from seemingly minor causes and the seriousness of the consequences are often a matter of chance. Any incident, though apparently trivial, should be regarded as a warning of something wrong in the system of work, the equipment used or the working area. Immediate attention should be given to remedying the defect or deficiency in order to avoid a repetition of the incident which might have more serious consequences.

2 Health and hygiene

2.1 It is the seafarer's responsibility to look after his own health and fitness. High standards of personal cleanliness and hygiene should be maintained.

2.2 Good health depends on an even and thoughtful balance of work, rest and active play, on sensible and regular meals, on adequate sleep and an avoidance of excesses of rich food, alcohol and tobacco.

2.3 On board ship, simple infections can easily be spread from one person to others. Thus preventive measures, as well as easily effective treatment, are essential.

2.4 Cuts and abrasions should be cleansed at once and given first aid treatment as necessary to protect against infection.

2.5 Many serious infections can be guarded against by inoculation and vaccination. These should be kept up to date as necessary to meet the requirements of the international voyages to be undertaken.

2.6 The risk of contracting malaria in certain parts of the world can be much reduced by taking precautions to avoid bites from mosquitoes carrying the disease, eg by the use of mosquito wire-screening and nets, keeping openings closed, and the use of anti-mosquito preparations or insecticides. Clothing also affords a degree of protection against mosquito bites and seafarers should therefore avoid going about after dusk with any part of the arms or legs exposed. The risk of infection should also be controlled by the taking of proguanil (Paludrine) by all members of the crew of a ship bound for a malarious port (see the *Ship Captain's Medical Guide*).

2.7 Barrier creams may help to protect exposed skin against dermatitis and also make thorough cleaning easier.

2.8 Prolonged exposure to mineral oils may cause dermatitis and skin cancer. All traces of oil should be thoroughly washed from the skin but hydrocarbon solvents should be avoided. Working clothes should be laundered frequently. Oil-soaked rags should not be put in pockets.

2.9 Anthrax is a dangerous disease. It can be contracted by handling the hides, wool, bristles, bones, horns, hooves or other products from infected animals and from any wrapping materials which have contained them. Overalls, head covering and protective gloves should be worn to protect the skin as far as possible. Fuller information is given in Guidance Note MS2 (Anthrax) published by the Health and Safety Executive (see Appendix 2).

2.10 Rats and other rodents may be carriers of infection and should never be handled, dead or alive, with bare hands.

2.11 Inadvertent exposure to or contact with toxic chemicals or other harmful substances should be reported immediately and the appropriate remedial action taken.

2.12 Prolonged exposure to synthetic domestic cleaners and detergents is a potential cause of alkali (de-fatting) dermatitis. Cotton-lined rubber or PVC gloves should be worn when using such substances.

2.13 Some domestic substances, for example caustic soda and bleaching powders or liquids, can burn the skin. They may react dangerously with other substances and ought not to be mixed indiscriminately.

2.14 High humidity and heat can lead to heat exhaustion and heat stroke which may be fatal. When working in these conditions it is advisable to drink at least 4.5 litres (8 pints) of cool (but not iced) water daily. It is best to take small quantities at frequent intervals. Extra salt is essential; this can be in the form of two salt tablets four times a day or a level tea-spoonful of table salt in plenty of water each morning and again in the evening, or added to food. If the work is in enclosed spaces, they should be well ventilated.

2.15 In tropical areas especially, exposure to the sun during the hottest part of the day should be avoided as far as possible. When it is necessary to work in very strong sunlight, appropriate clothing offering protection to both head and body should be worn, whatever the degree of acclimatisation may be.

2.16 Where it is required to work in exceptionally hot and/or humid conditions or when wearing respiratory equipment, it should be recognised that breaks at intervals in the fresh air or in the shade may be necessary.

2.17 Mis-use of alcohol or drugs affects a person's fitness for duty and harms his health. The immediate after-effects may increase liability to accidents. Drinking alcohol whilst under treatment with prescribed drugs should be avoided, since even common remedies such as aspirin, seasickness tablets or codeine may be dangerous in conjunction with alcohol.

2.18 As a general rule fresh fruit and salad should be thoroughly washed in fresh water before being eaten.

2.19 The inhalation of asbestos fibres, even in concentrations too low to be readily detectable, may cause serious lung disease or tumours. The risk is much greater for a person who smokes. Asbestos is commonly found in fire retardant bulkheads and thermal insulation, especially lagging, in packings, for example in the glands of high temperature valves, and in friction materials, especially brake linings. Wherever possible, work which might generate asbestos dust in the atmosphere should be left to be done when the ship is in port and proper facilities and equipment can be utilised. If it is essential for any such work to be done at sea, every precaution should be taken to keep the creation of asbestos dust at a minimum and to avoid risk of inhalation of fibres by persons on the ship:

(a) Access to areas where asbestos is being worked should be limited to those essential to the operation. When practicable, the working area should be closed off (by, for example, plastic sheeting) and suitable signs should be posted warning persons not wearing the appropriate protective clothing and equipment that they should not enter the area.

(b) Respiratory protective equipment, approved for the purpose by the Health & Safety Executive, which gives adequate protection against high concentrations of crocidolite (blue asbestos) dust should be worn by all persons undertaking such work (see Chapter 5, section 5). Full protective clothing should be worn comprising overalls and headgear, preferably of man-made fibre, which does not readily hold dust. The overalls should be close-fitting at the neck, ankles and wrists. Alternatively, disposable overalls may be worn provided they exclude asbestos dust.

(c) Work should be planned to ensure the least disturbance of the asbestos-containing material.

(d) Dust levels can be controlled or reduced by using approved portable dust extraction equipment, by using hand tools instead of power tools and by carefully handling and thoroughly wetting the material during the work to prevent the dust becoming airborne. The best method of removing lagging will depend upon the job in hand but where areas are large or exterior surfaces are non-absorbent, the material may have to be punctured to ensure thorough soaking.

(e) Where practicable, a plastic sheet should be used to collect all waste material as it is generated during the work. Waste material, and the plastic sheet, should be placed in polythene bags or other disposable impermeable receptacles which should then be tightly sealed for safe disposal ashore. All dust or other waste material should be thoroughly dampened before being swept up and placed in impermeable bags. The material used to 'close off' the working area, as recommended in (a), should also be properly disposed of in like fashion.

(f) Any edges or surfaces of asbestos materials left exposed by the work should be sealed or covered to prevent shedding of loose fibres.

(g) Contaminated protective clothing and equipment should, where possible, be vacuum-cleaned (using only a vacuum cleaner with a suitable filter) before being taken off or before the wearer enters 'uncontaminated' areas. On removal, the clothing should immediately be placed in a plastic bag, tape-sealed and clearly and boldly labelled 'Asbestos contaminated clothing' for separate laundering. If a suitable vacuum cleaner is not available, clothing should be taken off carefully to prevent the dust being disturbed and then placed in a dust-tight container as above.

(h) Parts of the body exposed whilst working with asbestos should be washed after removal of contaminated clothing.

(i) Any swabs or cloths used for cleaning up should not be left to dry out but should be thoroughly washed or, better still, sealed in impermeable bags for later safe disposal.

3 Working clothes

3.1 Clothing should be chosen to minimise working risks.

3.2 Working clothes should be close-fitting with no loose flaps, bulging pockets or ties, since injuries may result from clothing being caught up by moving parts of machinery or garments catching on obstructions or projections and causing falls. Clothing worn in galleys etc where there is a risk of burning or scalding should adequately cover the body to minimise this risk and be of a material of low flammability such as cotton or a cotton/terylene mix. Clothes should be kept in good repair.

3.3 Shirts or overalls provide better protection if they have long sleeves. Long sleeves should not be rolled up.

3.4 Scarves, sweat rags and other neck wear, loose clothing, finger rings and jewellery can be hazards when working with machinery. Long hair should be covered.

3.5 Sandals and plimsolls are dangerous and should not be worn when working, since they offer little protection against accidental scalds or burns or falling objects and add to the risks of tripping and falling or slipping on ladders (as do old, worn out, down-at-heel shoes). The wearing of appropriate industrial or safety footwear, which can be of good appearance, is recommended (see Chapter 5, section 6).

3.6 Gloves are a sensible precaution when handling sharp or hot objects but may easily be trapped on drum ends and in machinery. Whilst loose-fitting gloves allow hands to slip out readily, they do not give a good grip on ladders. Wet or oily gloves may be slippery and great care should be taken when working in them.

4 Shipboard housekeeping

4.1 Most of this Code deals with foreseeable risks arising in particular places and in performing particular jobs, but accidents may happen at any time in any part of the ship. Many such accidents can be prevented by always keeping things ship-shape and doing things in a seaman-like fashion, in the same way as a good standard of housekeeping produces a well-run, comfortable home on shore.

4.2 Wear and tear on a ship in service give rise to minor deficiencies in the structure, equipment or furnishings; for example, protruding nails and screws, loose fittings and handles, uneven and damaged flooring, rough and splintered edges to woodwork and jamming doors, any of which may cause cuts, bruises or trips and falls. They should be rectified immediately they are noticed.

4.3 If asbestos-containing panels, cladding or insulation work loose or are damaged in the course of a voyage, pending proper repair, the exposed edges or surfaces should be protected by a suitable coating or covering to prevent asbestos fibres being released and dispersed in the air (see also Chapter 1, section 2.19).

4.4 Flickering lights usually indicate faults in wiring or fittings which may cause electric shock or fires. They should be investigated and repaired by a competent person. Failed light bulbs should be replaced as soon as possible.

4.5 Instruction plates, notices and operating indicators should be kept clean and legible.

4.6 Heavy objects, particularly if at a height above deck level should be stowed securely against the movement of the ship or inadvertent displacement. Similarly, furniture etc likely to fall or shift during heavy weather should be properly secured.

4.7 Doors whether open or closed, should be properly secured; they should not be left swinging.

4.8 Litter may present a fire risk or cause slips or falls, but in any case may conceal some other hazard (see Chapter 2, section 4.1).

4.9 Tidiness not only makes hidden defects apparent but ensures that articles are in their proper place to be found as required.

4.10 In carrying out any task, possible risks to other persons should be considered; for example, if water from a careless hosing-down of the deck enters a galley through an open light or scuttle, it may be most dangerous to galley staff.

4.11 Care is needed in personal matters. Dangerous articles such as razor blades and lighted cigarette ends should be disposed of safely.

4.12 Many aerosols have volatile and inflammable contents. They should never be used or placed near naked flames or other heat source even when 'empty'. Empty canisters should be properly disposed of.

4.13 Some fumigating or insecticidal sprays contain ingredients which though perhaps in themselves harmless to human beings, may be decomposed when heated. Smoking may be dangerous in sprayed atmospheres while the spray persists.

CHAPTER 2

Fire precautions

The only sure way to avoid the disastrous consequences of a fire at sea is not to have one. All on board have therefore a personal interest in observing all practicable precautions against the outbreak of fire.

1 Smoking

1.1 Fires are often caused by the careless disposal of burning cigarette ends and matches. Ashtrays or other suitable containers should be provided and used at places where smoking is authorised. Care should be taken to ensure that matches are actually extinguished and cigarette ends properly stubbed out. They should not be thrown overboard since there is a danger that they may be blown back on board.

1.2 Conspicuous warning notices should be displayed in any part of the ship where smoking is forbidden (permanently or temporarily) and these should be obeyed in all circumstances.

1.3 It is dangerous to smoke in bed.

2 Electrical and other fittings

2.1 Unauthorised persons should not interfere with electrical fittings. Personal electrical appliances should be connected to the ship's supply only with the approval of the electrical officer or the responsible engineer officer. Notices should be displayed on the notice boards to this effect.

2.2 Faulty appliances, fittings or wiring which are part of the ship's equipment should be reported immediately to the head of department.

2.3 All electrical appliances should be firmly secured and served by permanent connections whenever possible.

2.4 Flexible leads should be as short as practicable and so arranged as to prevent their being chafed or cut in service.

2.5 Makeshift plugs, sockets and fuses should not be used.

2.6 Circuits should not be overloaded since this causes the wires to overheat, destroying insulation and thus resulting in a possible short-circuit which could start a fire.

2.7 All portable electrical appliances, lights etc should be isolated from the mains after use.

2.8 Personal portable space-heating appliances of any sort should not be used and notices to this effect should be displayed on notice boards.

3 Laundry and wet clothing

3.1 Clothing or other articles should not be placed over space heaters, or so close to heaters or light bulbs etc as to restrict the flow of air, and thus lead to overheating and fire (see also Chapter 26, section 5).

4 Spontaneous combustion

4.1 Dirty waste, rags, sawdust and other rubbish – especially if contaminated with oil – are dangerous if left lying about. Heat may be generated spontaneously within such rubbish which may be sufficient to ignite flammable mixtures or may become hot enough to set the rubbish itself on fire. Such waste and rubbish should therefore be properly stored until it can be safely disposed of as soon as possible thereafter.

4.2 Materials in ship's stores, including linen, blankets and similar absorbent materials are also liable to ignite by spontaneous combustion if damp or contaminated by oil. Strict vigilance, careful stowage and suitable ventilation are necessary to guard against such a possibility. If such materials become damp, they should be dried before being stowed away. If oil has soaked into them, they should be cleaned and dried, or destroyed. They should not be stowed in close proximity to oil or paints, or on or near to steam pipes.

5 Machinery spaces

5.1 The seriousness of fire in machinery spaces cannot be overstressed. All personnel should be fully aware of the precautions necessary for its prevention. Such precautions should include the maintenance of clean conditions, the prevention of oil leakage and the removal of all combustible materials from vulnerable positions (see Chapters 20 and 22).

5.2 Suitable metal containers should be provided for the storage of cotton waste, cleaning rags or similar materials after use. Such containers should be emptied at frequent intervals and the contents safely disposed of.

5.3 Wood, paints, spirits and tins of oil should not be kept in boiler rooms or machinery spaces.

5.4 All electric wiring should be well maintained and kept clean and dry. The rated load capacity of the wires and fuses should never be exceeded.

6 Galleys

6.1 Galleys and pantries present particular fire risks (see Chapter 25). Care should be taken in particular to avoid overheating or spilling fat or oil and to ensure that burners or heating plates are shut off when cooking is finished. Extractor flues and ranges etc should always be kept clean.

6.2 Means to smother fat or cooking oil fires, such as a fire blanket, should be readily available close to stoves.

7 Hot work

7.1 The precautions set out in Chapter 13, section 3 should be strictly followed to avoid the possibility of fire during welding, flame cutting or other hot work.

CHAPTER 3

Emergency procedures

1 Musters and drills

1.1 Musters and drills are required to be carried out regularly in accordance with the *Merchant Shipping (Musters) Rules 1965*, a copy of which is appended to this Chapter.

1.2 Musters and drills have the objective of preparing a trained and organised response to situations of great difficulty which may unexpectedly threaten loss of life at sea. It is important that they should be carried out realistically, approaching as closely as possible to emergency conditions. Changes in the ship's function and changes in the ship's personnel from time to time should be reflected in corresponding changes in the muster arrangements.

1.3 The muster list which has to be posted in conspicuous places in different parts of the ship before she sails may be supplemented either by individual cards issued to each member of the crew or by similar cards affixed to individual berths or bunks. The card should state the lifeboat or liferaft station at which the crew member should muster and his duties in the event of fire or emergency. The signals which will be used for emergency and boat stations musters should be clearly set out.

1.4 At the earliest opportunity after joining the ship, seamen should familiarise themselves with their emergency duties, the significance of the various alarm signals and the locations of their lifeboat station and of all lifesaving and firefighting equipment.

1.5 All the ship's personnel concerned should muster at a drill wearing lifejackets properly secured. The lifejackets should continue to be worn during lifeboat drills and launchings but in other cases they may subsequently be removed at the Master's discretion if they would impede or make unduly onerous the ensuing practice, provided they are kept ready to hand.

1.6 The timing of emergency drills should vary so that personnel who have not participated in a particular drill may take part in the next.

1.7 Any defects or deficiencies revealed during drills and the inspections which accompany them should be made good without delay.

2 Fire drills

2.1 Efficient fire-fighting demands the full co-operation of personnel in all departments of the ship. On hearing the fire signal, seamen should proceed immediately to carry out their assigned duties. Fire-fighting parties should assemble at their designated stations. Engine room personnel should start the fire pumps in machinery spaces and see that full pressure is put on fire mains. Any emergency pump situated outside machinery spaces should also be started; all members of the crew should know how to start and operate the pump.

2.2 The fire parties should be sent from their designated stations to the selected site of the supposed fire, taking with them emergency equipment such as axes and lamps and breathing apparatus. The locations should be changed in successive drills to give practice in differing conditions and in dealing with different types of fire so that accommodation, machinery spaces, store rooms, galleys and cargo holds or areas of high fire hazard are all covered from time to time.

2.3 An adequate number of hoses to deal with the assumed fire should be realistically deployed. At some stage in the drill, they should be tested by bringing them into use, firstly with water provided by the machinery space pump and secondly with water from the emergency pump alone.

2.4 The drill should extend, where practicable, to the testing and demonstration of the remote controls for ventilating fans, fuel pumps and fuel tank valves and the closing of openings.

2.5 Fixed fire extinguishing installations should be tested to the extent practicable.

2.6 Portable fire extinguishers should be available for demonstration of the manner of their use. They should include the different types applicable to different kinds of fire. At each drill, one extinguisher or more should be operated by a member of the fire party, a different member on each occasion. Extinguishers so used should be recharged before being returned to their normal location or sufficient spares should otherwise be carried for demonstration purposes.

2.7 Breathing apparatus should be worn by members of the fire-fighting parties so each member in turn has experience of its use. Search and rescue exercises should be undertaken in various parts of the ship. The apparatus should be cleaned and verified to be in good order before it is stowed; cylinders of self-contained breathing apparatus should be recharged or sufficient spare cylinders otherwise carried for this purpose.

2.8 Fire appliances, fire and watertight doors and other closing appliances and also fire detection and alarm systems which have not been used in the drill should be inspected to ensure that they are in good order, either at the time of the drill or immediately afterwards.

3 Survival craft drills

3.1 Arrangements for drills should take account of prevailing weather conditions.

3.2 Crew members taking part in lifeboat or liferaft drills should muster wearing warm outer clothing and lifejackets properly secured.

3.3 Where appropriate, the lowering gear and chocks should be inspected and a check made to ensure that all working parts are well lubricated.

3.4 When turning out davits or when bringing boats or rafts inboard under power, seamen should always keep clear of any moving parts.

3.5 The engines on motor lifeboats should be started and run ahead and astern. Care should be taken to avoid overheating the engine and the propeller shaft stern gland. All personnel should be familiar with the engine starting procedure.

3.6 Hand-operated mechanical propelling gear, if any, should be examined and similarly tested.

3.7 Radio equipment should be examined and tested, with the aerial erected, by the Radio Officer and the crew instructed in its use.

3.8 Water spray systems, where fitted, should be tested in accordance with the lifeboat manufacturer's instructions.

3.9 When a drill is held in port, as many as possible of the lifeboats and, where appropriate, liferafts should be cleared and swung out. Each boat should be lowered into the water at least once in every four months unless circumstances make it impracticable. Quick release mechanisms, where fitted, should be tested once the boat is water-borne.

3.10 Where the handle of the lifeboat winch would rotate during the operation of the winch, it should be removed before the boat is lowered on the brake or raised with an electric motor. If a handle cannot be removed, personnel should keep well clear of it.

3.11 Personnel in a craft being lowered should remain seated, keeping their hands inside the gunwale to avoid them being crushed against the ship's side. Lifejackets should be worn. Only the launching crew should remain in a craft being raised.

3.12 During drills, lifebuoys and lines should be readily available at the point of embarkation.

3.13 While craft are in the water, crews should practice manoeuvring the vessel by oar, sail or power as appropriate and should operate the water spray system where fitted on enclosed lifeboats.

3.14 Seamen should keep their fingers clear of the long-link when unhooking or securing blocks on to lifting hooks while the boat is in the water, and particularly if there is a swell.

3.15 Before craft in gravity davits are recovered by power, the operation of the limit switches or similar devices should be checked.

3.16 A portable hoist unit used to recover a craft should be provided with a crutch or have an attachment to resist the torque. These should be checked. If neither device is available, the craft should be raised by hand.

3.17 Where liferafts are carried, instruction should be given to the ship's personnel in their launching, handling and operation. Methods of boarding them and the disposition of equipment and stores on them should be explained.

3.18 The statutory scale of lifesaving appliances must be maintained at all times. If the use of a liferaft for practice would bring equipment below the specified scale, a replacement must first be made available.

4 Action in the event of fire

4.1 The risk of fire breaking out on board a ship cannot be eliminated but will be much reduced if the advice given elsewhere in the Code is conscientiously followed at all times (see Chapter 2).

4.2 Training in fire-fighting procedures and maintenance of equipment should be assured by regular drills in accordance with section 2 of this Chapter, but it is important also that access to fire-fighting equipment should be kept unimpeded at all times and that emergency escapes and passage ways are never obstructed.

4.3 A fire in its first few minutes can usually be readily extinguished; prompt and correct action is essential.

4.4 If fire breaks out, the alarm should be raised and the bridge informed immediately. If the ship is in port, the local fire authority should be called. If possible, an attempt should be made to extinguish or limit the fire, by any appropriate means readily available, either using suitable portable extinguishers or by smothering the fire as in the instance of a fat or oil fire in a galley.

4.5 The different types of portable fire extinguishers on board are appropiate to different kinds of fire. Water extinguishers should not be used on oil or electrical fires.

4.6 Openings to the space should be shut to reduce the supply of air to the fire and to prevent it spreading. Any fuel lines feeding the fire or threatened by it should be isolated. If practicable, combustible materials adjacent to the fire should be removed.

4.7 If a space is filling with smoke and fumes, personnel, unless properly equipped with breathing apparatus, should get out of the space without delay; if necessary, escape should be effected by crawling on hands and knees because air close to deck level is likely to be relatively clear.

4.8 After a fire has been extinguished, precautions should be taken against its spontaneous re-ignition.

4.9 Personnel, unless wearing breathing apparatus, should not re-enter a space in which a fire has occurred before it has been fully ventilated.

STATUTORY INSTRUMENTS

1965 No. 1113

MERCHANT SHIPPING

SAFETY

The Merchant Shipping (Musters) Rules 1965

Made - - - -	11*th May* 1965
Laid before Parliament	19*th May* 1965
Coming into Operation	26*th May* 1965

The Board of Trade in exercise of their powers under Section 427 of the Merchant Shipping Act 1894(**a**) as substituted by Section 2 of the Merchant Shipping (Safety Convention) Act 1949(**b**) and as having effect by virtue of the Transfer of Functions (Shipping and Construction of Ships) Order 1965(**c**) and of all other powers enabling them in that behalf hereby make the following Rules:—

Interpretation and Repeal

1.—(1) These Rules shall come into operation on the 26th May 1965 and may be cited as the Merchant Shipping (Musters) Rules 1965.

(2) In these Rules, unless the context otherwise requires, the expression " muster " includes a boat-drill and a fire-drill.

(3) These Rules apply to—

(*a*) British ships, except ships registered in a Dominion within the meaning of the Statute of Westminster 1931 or in India, Pakistan, Ceylon, Ghana, Malaysia, the Republic of Cyprus, Nigeria, Sierra Leone, Tanzania, Jamaica, Trinidad and Tobago, Uganda, Kenya, Malawi, Malta, Zambia, The Gambia, the Republic of Ireland, or in any territory administered by Her Majesty's Government in any such Dominion;

(*b*) other ships while they are within any port in the United Kingdom.

Provided that these Rules shall not apply to a ship by reason of her being within a port in the United Kingdom if she would not have been in any such port but for stress of weather or any other circumstance that neither the master nor the owner nor the charterer (if any) of the ship could have prevented or forestalled.

(4) The Interpretation Act 1889(**d**), shall apply to the interpretation of these Rules as it applies to the interpretation of an Act of Parliament and as if these Rules and the Rules hereby revoked were Acts of Parliament.

(5) The Merchant Shipping (Musters) Rules 1952(**e**) are hereby revoked.

Classification of Ships

2. For the purposes of these Rules the ships to which these Rules apply shall be arranged in the same classes in which ships are arranged for the purposes of the Merchant Shipping (Life-Saving Appliances) Rules 1965(**f**), and any reference in these Rules to a ship of any class shall be construed accordingly.

(**a**) 57 & 58 Vict. c. 60. (**b**) 12, 13 & 14 Geo. 6. c. 43. (**c**) S.I. 1965/145 (1965 I, p. 438).
(**d**) 52 & 53 Vict. c. 63. (**e**) S.I. 1952/1951 (1952 II, p. 1927). (**f**) S.I. 1965/1105.

Muster List

3.—(1) The Master of every ship of Classes I, II, II(A), III, VII, VII(A) and VIII shall prepare a muster list showing in respect of each member of the crew the special duties which are allotted to him and the station or stations to which he shall go in the event of an emergency (hereinafter referred to as "emergency station" or "emergency stations").

(2) The muster list shall specify definite signals, to be made on the whistle or siren, for calling all the crew to their emergency stations and in passenger ships one of such signals shall be the signal required by Rule 4(2) of these Rules. In ships of Class I and in ships of 150 feet in length or over of Classes VII, VII(A) and VIII, such signals shall be supplemented by other means of warning which shall be electrically operated and which shall be capable of being operated from the bridge. The muster list shall also specify the means of indicating when the ship is to be abandoned.

(3) The muster list shall show the duties assigned to the different members of the crew in connection with—

(*a*) The closing of the watertight doors, fire doors, sidescuttles, valves and closing mechanism of scuppers, ash-shoots, or other similar openings in the ship's side;

(*b*) The equipping of the boats and other life-saving appliances;

(*c*) The launching of the boats and liferafts attached to davits or to other launching appliances;

(*d*) General preparations of any other boats and other life-saving appliances;

(*e*) The muster of the passengers (if any); and

(*f*) The extinction of fire.

(4) The duty of seeing that the boats and other life-saving appliances are at all times ready for use shall be specified in the muster list as the duty of one or more officers.

(5) The muster list shall show the several duties assigned to the members of the stewards' department in relation to the passengers at a time of emergency.

These duties shall include—

(*a*) Warning the passengers;

(*b*) Seeing that they are suitably clad and have put on their lifejackets in a proper manner;

(*c*) Assembling the passengers at muster stations;

(*d*) Keeping order in the passages and on the stairways and generally controlling the movements of the passengers; and

(*e*) Seeing that a supply of blankets is taken to the lifeboats.

(6) The muster list shall be prepared, or, if a new list is not necessary, revised after the agreement with the crew has been signed and before the ship proceeds to sea, and shall be dated and signed by the Master.

(7) If after the muster list has been prepared, any change takes place in the crew which necessitates an alteration in the muster list, the Master shall either revise the list or prepare a new list.

(8) Copies of the muster list shall be posted in several parts of the ship, and in particular in the crew's quarters, before the ship proceeds to sea and shall be kept so posted while the ship is at sea.

2

Emergency Signal for Passengers

4.—(1) Muster stations for all passengers shall be appointed for the event of an emergency and the position of those stations and the meaning of all signals affecting passengers, with precise instructions as to what they are to do, shall be clearly stated in English and such other languages as are appropriate on cards posted in their cabins and in conspicuous places in other passenger quarters.

(2) The emergency signal for summoning passengers to the muster stations shall be a succession of seven or more short blasts followed by one long blast on the whistle or siren. In ships of Class I this signal shall be supplemented by other means of warning audible throughout the ship which shall be electrically operated and capable of being operated from the bridge.

Training

5.—(1) In ships of Class I a muster of the crew shall be held before the ship leaves her final port of departure in the United Kingdom and a muster of the passengers, embarked at any port, shall be held within twenty-four hours after leaving such port.

(2) In ships of Classes I, II, II(A) and III, musters of the crew shall take place at intervals of not more than seven days, when practicable, to ensure that the crew understand and are drilled in the duties assigned to them for the event of an emergency.

(3) In ships of Classes VII, VII(A), VIII, VIII(A), IX and in ships of Class X of 70 feet in length or over and in ships of Class XI which proceed beyond Home Trade limits, musters of the crew shall take place at intervals of not more than fourteen days, and if more than 25 per cent of the crew have been replaced at any port, one of such musters shall take place within 24 hours of leaving that port. In all other ships of Classes X and XI the Master shall take steps to ensure that the crew understand the uses of the life-saving equipment and fire appliances on board and know where they are kept.

(4) Different groups of boats shall be used in turn at successive boat drills so that every lifeboat shall be swung out at least once a month and, if practicable and reasonable, lowered at least once every four months. The musters and inspections shall be so arranged that the crew thoroughly understand and are practised in the duties they have to perform, and that all life-saving appliances and fire appliances with the gear appertaining to them are always ready for immediate use.

(5) The Master shall take steps to ensure that the crew are properly instructed in the handling and operation of the liferafts on board.

11th May 1965.

Roy Mason,
Minister of State,
Board of Trade.

EXPLANATORY NOTE

(This Note is not part of the Rules.)

These Rules supersede the Merchant Shipping (Musters) Rules 1952.

Ships are arranged into classes for the purposes of the Rules, the classification being uniform with that in the Merchant Shipping (Life-Saving Appliances) Rules 1965. The Rules provide for the assignment of the duties to be performed by members of the crew in case of emergency, for training in those duties and for the emergency signal for passengers. The Rules include such provisions as appear to the Board of Trade to implement the provisions of the International Convention for the Safety of Life at Sea 1960 relating to musters.

Printed in England by Oyez Press Limited, and published by Her Majesty's Stationery Office
22/P13752 V13 K8 11/75

Reprinted 1975

12p net

ISBN 0 11 100246 X

CHAPTER 4

Safety officers and safety committees

1 General

1.1 The Master is responsible for the overall safety of the ship and of all those on board her. Under him each individual member of the ship's crew has a duty to ensure safety in those matters within his own control, whether supervising or carrying out a task, or in reporting or remedying defects which might impair safety. All the safeguards and other facilities provided for the safety of the seafarer should be used.

1.2 The development of the necessary degree of safety consciousness and the achievement of high standards of safety depend on foresight, good organisation and the whole-hearted support of all members of the crew. It is therefore important that arrangements should exist on every ship whereby the ship's complement can co-operate and participate in establishing and maintaining safe working conditions. This can be achieved by the appointment of a Safety Officer with appropriate functions and, in suitable circumstances, a Safety Committee.

2 Safety Officers

2.1 The ship's Safety Officer may be drawn from any section of the crew but it is important that he has adequate length of experience in work on board ship and has had proper training for the purpose.

2.2 The Safety Officer's responsibilities should extend to all departments of the ship but he should always work in close co-operation and consultation with the respective heads of department and with the Safety Committee where one is established.

2.3 The Safety Officer's role should be a positive one in that he should seek to initiate or develop safety measures before an accident occurs rather than afterwards. He should advise the Master on all matters of safe working practice and assist him in the elimination of accidents and injuries on board ship by:

(a) fostering among the ship's complement a high degree of safety consciousness and an active interest in accident prevention;

(b) providing a channel by which suggestions for improving safety may be transmitted from seagoing personnel to management;

(c) ensuring general compliance with safety instructions and safety rules, including this Code of Safe Working Practices;

(d) investigating any accidents and unsafe occurrences, working practices or conditions on the ship.

2.4 In carrying out these functions, the Safety Officer should, with the approval of or at the direction of the Master:

(a) arrange the distribution of booklets, leaflets and similar advisory and informative material concerning safety matters;

(b) supervise the display of posters and notices and their replacement or renewal in due time;

(c) arrange for the showing of films of safety publicity and, where appropriate, organise subsequent discussions on the subjects depicted;

(d) encourage members of the crew to submit ideas and suggestions for improving safety and enlist their support for any proposed safety measures which may affect them. The person making a suggestion should always be informed of decisions reached and any action taken;

(e) consider any other ways of creating and maintaining interest in improving safety;

(f) receive and draw attention as appropriate to relevant shipping legislation, Department of Trade Merchant Shipping Notices and company and ship's rules and instructions relating to safety of work about the ship. Special regard should be had for persons new on the ship and their attention should always be drawn to any special hazards on the ship;

(g) make inspections to detect unsafe conditions, fire hazards, and unsafe practices, for example, unguarded openings, slippery floors, bad lighting, accumulations of rubbish, defects or deficiencies in equipment and failures to use safe equipment where it is needed. It is preferable to make a thorough inspection of one area or department on each occasion rather than attempt a cursory inspection of the whole ship;

(h) act on any reported or observed defects, deficiencies and unsafe conditions with recommendations for action to deal with them;

(i) consider any apparent unsafe procedures arising from lack of supervision or instruction, or instances of slackness or carelessness in working habits and practices, to find ways of dealing with the problems so that appropriate recommendations may be made;

(j) study any accidents or dangerous occurrences that have happened, determine causes, identify practical precautions which would prevent repetition and report to the Master. In no case, should an attempt be made to apportion blame to any person or persons;

(k) maintain an accident record book, summarising the conclusions reached on every accident and dangerous occurrence studied, in order to provide a permanent source of guidance to later Safety Officers about specially hazardous areas and operations on the ship.

2.5 In assigning duties to a Safety Officer, full consideration should be given to his other duties.

3 Safety Committees

3.1 Where a Safety Committee is also established on a ship, it is important to ensure that all departments are adequately represented. The Master (or his representative) should be Chairman, a Secretary should be appointed and the ship's Safety Officer should be a member. The Committee should be reasonably compact in order to function efficiently.

3.2 Passenger ships may have large numbers of staff working in kitchens, galleys, restaurants and dining saloons. In these and similar instances, sub-committees should be formed on lines similar to those recommended for the main committee but confined to the department and under the chairmanship of a senior member of the department who should serve as a member of the main safety committee in order to report the views of the sub-committee.

3.3 On short-haul ferries on which different crews work a shift system, some enlargement of the Committee may have to be accepted as the only practicable means of securing proper representation, but a scheme of alternate members may be found satisfactory.

3.4 In all cases, the choice of the officers' and ratings' representatives should be left to the decision of those groups, but it is desirable that any chosen representative should have had adequate experience to enable him to contribute properly to the work of the Safety Committee. Normally two years' sea service as an officer or an adult rating would be the minimum to provide the necessary experience.

3.5 The Safety Committee should meet at such intervals as circumstances dictate and in any case sufficiently frequently to ensure that matters are not overlooked.

3.6 An agenda giving notice of a meeting should be issued in advance of the meeting together with copies of any documents, papers etc to be discussed. Committee members should be encouraged to suggest items to be discussed.

3.7 Minutes of each meeting should record concisely the business discussed and conclusions reached. A copy should be provided to each Committee member. Normally, they should be agreed as a true record at the next meeting, or amended if necessary, under the first item of the agenda. Matters arising from the minutes would be taken as the next item on the agenda, unless featuring as separate items on the agenda.

3.8 A Minutes File or Book should be maintained, together with a summary of recommendations recording conclusions reached, in order to provide a permanent source of reference and so ensuring continuity should there be changes in the personnel serving on the Committee.

3.9 The ship's complement should be kept informed on matters of interest which have been discussed by summaries or extracts from the minutes posted on the ship's notice board. Suggestions may be stimulated by similarly posting the agenda in advance of meetings.

3.10 Relevant extracts of agreed minutes should be forwarded through the Master to the Company even though certain matters therein may have been already taken up with them.

3.11 The Safety Committee should work in close liaison with the Safety Officer and undertake any of the functions prescribed in section 2 as agreed with him.

4 Responsibilities of ships' management

4.1 Managements have the responsibility for supporting the work of Safety Officers and Committees by taking an active and constant interest in the work and helping where they can to make it effective. Managements should designate a person ashore to be responsible for ensuring that their safety policy is pursued and to receive reports by ships' Safety Officers or of Safety Committees' meetings which should be studied and, where appropriate, recommendations acted on. Where action is not considered appropriate or cannot be taken within a reasonable period of time, or the form of remedial action cannot be agreed, then the reasons should be explained to those making the recommendation.

4.2 Managers should also ensure that all seafarers in the ships under their supervision are provided with information on matters affecting their health and safety at work and, in addition, should make available to appointed Safety Officers and Safety Committees such further information which they may need to enable them to carry out their functions properly. Such information should include that of a technical nature about the hazards and precautions deemed necessary to eliminate or minimise them, in respect of machinery, plant, equipment, processes, systems of work and substances in use at work, or carried as cargo (where these matters are not already covered by official regulations), including relevant information provided by the designer, manufacturer, importer or supplier of any article or substance used by their employees, or carried on their ships.

4.3 Where an accident or dangerous occurrence has been reported by a Master, consideration should be given to warning other ships of the occurrence together with appropriate recommendations on action to be taken.

CHAPTER 5

Protective clothing and equipment

1 General

1.1 Overalls, gloves and suitable footwear should be the proper working dress for most work about the ship but these may not give adequate protection against particular hazards in certain jobs.

1.2 Specific recommendations for the use of special protective clothing and equipment will be found in certain sections of the Code but there will be other occasions when such special protection is necessary and these can only be determined at the time by the officer in charge of the particular operation.

1.3 Protective clothing or equipment does nothing to reduce the hazard, it merely sets up a frail barrier against it. The first step in injury prevention should be the elimination of the hazards to the extent that is reasonable and practicable. Personal protective clothing and equipment should be relied upon to afford protection against the hazards that remain.

1.4 Defective or ineffective protective equipment provide no defence. It is therefore essential that the correct items of equipment are selected and that they are properly maintained at all times. The manufacturer's instructions should be kept safe with the relevant apparatus and when necessary referred to before use and when maintenance is carried out. The equipment should be kept clean and should be disinfected as and when necessary for health reasons.

1.5 A responsible officer should inspect each item of protective equipment at regular intervals and in all cases before and after use. He should ensure that it is returned and properly stowed in a safe place. Personal protective clothing and equipment should always be checked by the wearer each time before use.

1.6 All personnel who may be required to use protective equipment should be properly trained in its use and advised of its limitations.

1.7 Personal protective clothing and equipment can be classified as follows: Head protection: safety helmets, hair protection. Hearing protection. Face and eye protection: goggles and spectacles, facial shields. Respiratory protective equipment: dust masks, respirators, breathing apparatus. Hand and foot protection: gloves, safety boots and shoes. Body protection: safety suits, safety belts, harnesses, aprons.

2 Head protection

Safety helmets

2.1 Objects falling from a height present a hazard against which safety helmets are most commonly provided. Other hazards include abnormal heat, risk of a sideways blow or crushing, or chemical splashes. These four different types of common risk are given as a guide only and are not intended to be comprehensive.

2.2 Since the hazards are so varied in type it will be appreciated that no one type of helmet would be ideal as protection in every case. Design details are normally decided by the manufacturer whose primary consideration will be compliance with an appropriate Standard (see Appendix 1).

2.3 The shell of a helmet should be of one piece seamless construction designed to resist impact. The harness or suspension when properly adjusted forms a cradle for supporting the protector on the wearer's head. The crown straps help absorb the force of impact. They are designed to permit a clearance of approximately 25 mm between the shell and the skull of the wearer. The harness or suspension should be properly adjusted before a helmet is worn.

Bump caps

2.4 A bump cap is simply an ordinary cap with a hard penetration-resistant shell. They are useful as a protection against bruising and abrasion when working in confined spaces such as a main engine crankcase or a double bottom tank. They do not, however, afford the same protection as safety helmets and are intended only to protect against minor knocks.

Hair nets and safety caps
2.5 Personnel working on or near to moving machinery have always to be on their guard against the possibility of loose clothing, jewellery, or their hair becoming entangled in the machinery. Not only should particular attention be given to the guarding of all moving machine parts, but it is equally important to ensure that the added risks mentioned above are avoided. In the case of long hair, hair nets or safety caps should be worn where any risk of entanglement exists.

3 Hearing protection

3.1 All persons exposed to high levels of noise, eg in machinery spaces, should wear ear protectors of a type recommended as suitable for the particular circumstances. Protectors are of three types – ear plugs, disposable or permanent, and ear muffs. For further information see the code of practice *Noise Levels in Ships*, published by the Department of Trade.

3.2 The simplest form of ear protection is the glass-down ear plug. This type however has the disadvantage of limited capability of noise level reduction. Ear plugs of rubber or plastic also have only limited effect, in that extremes of high or low frequency cause the plug to vibrate in the ear canal causing a consequential loss in protection.

3.3 In general, ear muffs provide a more effective form of hearing protection. They consist of a pair of rigid cups designed to completely envelope the ears, fitted with soft sealing rings to fit closely against the head around the ears. The ear cups are connected by a spring loaded headband (or neck band) which ensures that the sound seals around the ears are maintained. Different types are available and provision should be made according to the circumstances of use and expert advice on suitability therefor.

4 Face and eye protection

4.1 In selecting eye and combined eye and face protectors, careful consideration should be given to the kind and degree of the hazard, and the degree of protection and comfort afforded.

4.2 The main causes of eye injury are:
(a) infra-red rays – gas welding;
(b) ultra-violet rays – electric welding;
(c) exposure to chemicals;
(d) exposure to particles and foreign bodies.
Protectors are available in a wide variety, designed to BS specifications, to protect against these different types of hazard (see Appendix 1).

4.3 Ordinary prescription (corrective) spectacles, unless manufactured to a safety standard, do not afford protection. Certain box-type goggles are designed so that they can be worn over ordinary spectacles.

5 Respiratory protective equipment

5.1 Respiratory protective equipment of the appropriate type is essential for protection when work has to be done in conditions of irritating, dangerous or poisonous dust, fumes or gases. The equipment may be either a respirator, which filters the air before it is breathed, or breathing apparatus which supplies air or oxygen from an uncontaminated source. The selection of the correct respiratory protective equipment for any given situation requires consideration of the nature of the hazard, the severity of the hazard, work requirements and conditions, and the characteristics and limitations of available equipment. Advice on selection and the use and maintenance of the equipment is contained in the relevant British Standard, which should be available to all those concerned with the use of respiratory protective equipment on board ship (see Appendix 1).

5.2 It is most important that the facepiece incorporated in respirators and breathing apparatus is fitted correctly to prevent leakage. The wearing of spectacles, unless adequately designed for the purpose, and beards and whiskers are likely to adversely affect the face seal.

Respirators

5.3 The respirator selected must be of a type designed to protect against the hazards being met.

5.4 The most common type is the dust respirator, affording protection against dusts and aerosol sprays but not against gases. There are many types of dust respirator available but they are generally of the ori-nasal type, ie half-masks covering the nose and mouth. Many types of light, simple face masks are also available. which are extremely useful for protecting against dust nuisance and non-toxic sprays but should never be used in place of proper protection against harmful dusts or sprays.

5.5 The positive pressure powered dust respirator incorporates a face-piece connected by a tube to a battery-powered blower unit carried by the wearer to create a positive pressure in the face-piece and thus make breathing easier and reduce face-seal leakage.

5.6 The cartridge-type of respirator consists of a full face-piece or half mask connected to a replaceable cartridge containing absorbent or adsorbent material and a particulate filter. It is designed to provide protection against low concentrations of certain relatively non-toxic gases and vapours.

5.7 The canister-type of respirator incorporates a full face-piece connected to an absorbent or adsorbent material contained in a replaceable canister carried in a sling on the back or side of the wearer. This type gives considerably more protection than the cartridge type.

5.8 The filters, canisters and cartridges incorporated in respirators are designed to provide protection against certain specified dusts or gases. Different types are available to provide protection against different hazards and it is therefore important that the appropriate type is selected for the particular circumstances or conditions being encountered. It must be remembered, however, that they have a limited effective life and must be replaced or renewed at intervals in accordance with manufacturers' instructions.

5.9 Respirators provide NO protection against oxygen deficient atmospheres. They should never be used to provide protection in confined spaces such as tanks, cofferdams, double bottoms or other similar spaces against dangerous fumes, gases or vapours. Breathing apparatus only (self-contained or airline) is capable of giving protection in such circumstances (see Chapter 10).

Breathing apparatus

5.10 Self-contained breathing apparatus used on board ship is of the open-circuit type comprising full face-piece connected by a tube to a cylinder of compressed air via a demand valve and/or a pressure reducer, the cylinder being carried by the wearer in a harness on his back. Properly used, this apparatus is safe for use in any toxic atmosphere or in an area deficient in oxygen, but the period of protection is strictly limited by the capacity of the cylinder.

5.11 Breathing apparatus should not be used under water unless the equipment is suitable for the purpose, and then only in an emergency.

5.12 Air line breathing apparatus has a face-piece connected either to a source of uncontaminated air by a hose or is connected by way of a reducing valve and filter to a source of clean compressed air. The hose is suitable for use only over a short distance, not exceeding 9 metres (30 ft), unless the air supply hose is under pressure.

5.13 The practice of two or more persons wearing airline breathing apparatus all being connected to a single air supply hose is unsafe.

Resuscitators

5.14 Resuscitators of an appropriate kind should be carried on all ships.

6 Hand and foot protection

Gloves

6.1 The correct type of gloves should be chosen according to the hazard being faced and the kind of work being undertaken, for example, leather gloves are generally best when handling rough or sharp objects, heat-resistant gloves when handling hot objects, and rubber, synthetic or PVC gloves when handling acids, alkalis, various types of oils, solvents and chemicals in general. The exact type selected will depend upon the particular substance being handled, and in these cases expert advice should be followed (see also Chapter 1, section 3.6).

Footwear

6.2 Foot injuries most often result from the wearing of unsuitable footwear rather than from failure to wear safety shoes or boots. It is nevertheless strongly advisable that all personnel whilst at work on board ship, wear appropriate safety footwear.

6.3 The hazards commonly encountered cause injury as a result of impact, penetration through the sole, slipping, heat and crushing. Safety footwear is available which is designed to protect against these or other specific hazards, manufactured to various British Standards appropriate to the particular danger involved (see Appendix 1).

7 Protection from falls

7.1 All seamen who are working aloft, outboard or below decks or in any other area where there is a risk of falling more than 2 metres, should wear a safety harness (or belt with shock absorber) attached to a lifeline.

7.2 Inertial clamp devices allow more freedom in movement.

8 Body protection

8.1 Special outerwear may be needed for protection when the seaman is exposed to contact with particular contaminating or corrosive substances. This apparel should be kept for the particular purpose and dealt with as directed in the relevant sections of this Code.

CHAPTER 6

Signs, notices and colour codes

1 General

1.1 Colours and symbols appropriately used can provide ever-present information and warnings of hazards which are essential to safety at work, and in some instances may be independent of language. The following provisions are intended to institute a uniform system on ships of United Kingdom registry to the extent that it is practicable to do so, bearing in mind that work is still being carried through in harmonising systems internationally. Those having vision in any way deficient in colour perception should take appropriate care where colour is used as a sole means of identification.

2 Signs and notices

2.1 Safety signs and notices should conform in shape and colour with the relevant British Standard Specification (see Appendix 1). If there is a need to amplify or clarify the meaning of any symbols used in these signs and notices, then an appropriate text, for example, 'Not Drinking Water', should be given in black below the sign.

2.2 Signs of prohibition should be based on a red circular band and red diagonal bar running through the left upper quadrant to the lower right quadrant, with white backing. The symbol for the prohibited action should be shown in black behind the red diagonal bar, for example, 'No Smoking' with a cigarette depicted.

2.3 Signs reminding of an essential precaution should comprise a blue disc upon which is superimposed in white a symbol of the precaution to be taken or appropriate wording, for example 'Goggles to be Worn' with a man's head with goggles depicted.

2.4 Warning signs should be based on a yellow triangle bordered by a black band; the symbol for the hazard is depicted in black, for example, poisoning risk with black skull and crossed bones on the yellow background.

2.5 Information of a safety nature should be shown by words or a symbol in white upon a green square or rectangle, for example, a white arrow on a green background points to an emergency exit. The same principle applies to fire-fighting equipment and its location except that the background colour should be red.

3 Portable fire extinguishers

3.1 There is no national standard for the colour coding of fire extinguishers in respect of their contents, but water-type extinguishers are invariably painted red.

3.2 Where colour coding is used by manufacturers to indicate the fire extinguishing medium contained in the extinguisher, it will usually be as follows:

Water	– Signal Red
Foam	– Pale Cream
Powder (all types)	– French Blue
Carbon Dioxide	– Black
Halon	– Emerald Green

4 Electrical wiring

4.1 The cores of electrical cables should be identifiable throughout their length by readily identifiable colours or numbers. Although various Standards (British, other national and international) exist for colour coding of cores, the colours specified in the standards differ. The colours found on any ship will therefore depend on the country of building or of manufacture of the cables. Care should therefore always be taken to make a positive identification of cable duty, and colours should be used primarily as a means of conductor tracing.

4.2 Particular care is required when connecting plugs to domestic equipment which has been brought on to a ship, as a wrong connection may prove fatal. New British equipment should now be supplied with cable to the new international standard, ie brown for 'live', blue for 'neutral' and yellow/green for 'earth', but older equipment and that purchased abroad may have other colours.

5 Gas cylinders

5.1 Gas cylinders used on United Kingdom ships should be marked and colour coded according to the relevant British Standard Specification (see Appendix 1).

5.2 Each cylinder should be clearly marked with the name of the gas and its chemical formula or symbol. The cylinder body should be coloured according to contents, with, where necessary, a secondary colour band painted around the neck of the cylinder to denote the particular hazards of the gas (flammability, toxicity, etc). Examples of such colour coding on gas cylinders commonly used on board ship are as follows:

Name of gas	Chemical formula or symbol	Ground colour of container	Colour of band
Oxygen	O_2	Black	None
Carbon Dioxide	CO_2	Black	None
Compressed Air	None (mixed gases)	French Grey	None
Nitrogen	N_2	French Grey	Black
Acetylene	C_2H_2	Maroon	None
Propane	None (mixed gases)	Signal Red	None
Butane	None (mixed gases)	None Specified	Signal Red

Note Cylinders of refrigerant gases are not allocated specific ground or band colours under the British Standard Specification.

5.3 Medical gas cylinders carried on board should similarly be marked in accordance with the relevant British Standard Specification (see Appendix 1). The name of the gas or gas mixture contained in the cylinder should be shown on a label affixed to it. The chemical symbol of the gas should be given on the shoulder of the cylinder. The cylinder should also be colour-coded according to contents as shown in the following examples:

Name of gas	Symbol	Colour of body	Colour of valve end
Oxygen	O_2	Black	White
Compressed Air (for breathing app)	AIR	Grey	White and Black

6 Pipelines

6.1 The following colour coding system is recommended for adoption for the main common pipeline services on United Kingdom registered ships:

Pipe contents	Basic identification colour	BS colour reference BS 4800	Colour code band	BS colour reference BS 4800
Water (Fresh)	Green	12D 45	Blue	18E 53
Water (Salt)	Green	12D 45	None	
Water (Fire Extinguishing)	Green	12D 45	Safety Red	04E 53
Compressed Air	Light Blue	20E 51	None	
Steam	Silver Grey	10A 03	None	
Oil (Diesel Fuel)	Brown	06C 39	White	—
Oil (Furnace Fuel)	Brown	06C 39	None	
Oil (Lubricating)	Brown	06C 39	Emerald Green	14E 53

6.2 The basic identification colour should be applied on the pipe either over its whole length or as a colour band at regular intervals along the pipe. The colour should similarly be applied at junctions, both sides of valves, service appliances, bulkheads etc, or at any other place where identification might be necessary. Valves on pipelines used for firefighting should be painted red.

6.3 Where applicable, the colour code banding should be in approximately 100 mm widths at regular intervals along the length of the pipe on the basic identification colour or painted between two basic identification colour bands each of a width of about 150 mm as shown in the following examples:

Pipe contents	Basic colour (150 mm approx)	Colour code (100 mm approx)	Basic colour (150 mm (approx)
Water (Fresh)	Green	Blue	Green
Water (Fire Extinguishing)	Green	Safety Red	Green
Diesel Fuel	Brown	White	Brown

6.4 Care should be taken to ensure that when replacing or repainting pipes, valves etc, the correct colour is used.

6.5 When it is necessary to know the direction of flow of the fluid, this should be indicated by an arrow situated in the proximity of the basic identification colour and painted white or black in order to contrast clearly with that colour.

6.6 Such a system as recommended above would be useful, for instance, in tracing a run of pipes but should not be relied upon as a positive identification of the contents of the pipe; a check should always be made before opening up and precautions taken against the contingency that the content is other than that expected.

6.7 Other pipeline systems on ships, such as cargo pipelines, may be colour-coded in a similar fashion but no specific recommendations are made here because a comprehensive system to cover the needs of all types of ship would require so wide a range of colours that contrasts would be small and easily obscured by fading or dirt.

6.8 Colour coding of pipelines may vary from ship to ship and seamen moving from one ship to another should ascertain from a competent officer what the colours mean on each particular vessel.

7 Dangerous goods

7.1 All dangerous goods and substances carried as cargo on ships have to be classified, packed and labelled in accordance with the Merchant Shipping (Dangerous Goods) Rules as set out in the current edition of the Report of the Department of Trade Standing Advisory Committee on the Carriage of Dangerous Goods in Ships (the 'Blue Book').

7.2 Examples of the labels to be affixed to packages and containers of dangerous goods, depicting by colour, name and 'hazard diagram', the particular dangers of that substance (flammability, toxicity, corrosiveness etc) are given in Appendix C of the 'Blue Book' and in the International Maritime Dangerous Goods Code.

CHAPTER 7

Permit-to-work systems

1 There are many types of operation on board ship where the routine actions of one man may inadvertently endanger another or when a series of action steps need to be taken to ensure the safety of those engaged in a specific operation. Danger may arise from the activation of a radar installation while men are working in the vicinity of the scanner; unusual risks may arise during the repair and maintenance work when in-built safeguards, effective during normal operation, have to be disturbed; a number of safety measures and precautions need to be taken before work is done in a tank or duct keel.

2 In all instances, it is necessary before the work is begun, to identify the hazards and then to ensure that they are eliminated or effectively controlled. Sometimes automatic safeguards on machinery or electrical equipment, for example, may greatly reduce the hazards but normally reliance has to be placed on the people involved following a proper procedure. In those cases verbal instructions, requests and responses which might be misheard, misinterpreted or not fully remembered are not a satisfactory basis for activities in which men's lives may be at risk. A more effective control can be achieved by the use of a written system which requires step by step formal actions by those responsible for the work. Such a system may be instituted by use of a 'permit-to-work'. That essentially is a document which sets out the work to be done, and the precautions to be taken in doing it. It consists basically of an organised and pre-defined safety procedure. It forms a clear record of all the foreseeable hazards which have been considered in advance and the appropriate precautions which have been determined and shows the correct sequence of operations and precautions. A permit-to-work does not in itself make the job safe, but is a guide dependent for its effectiveness upon the conscientious observance of the set procedure by those involved in the job.

3 The particular circumstances of individual ships will determine the particular areas in which permit-to-work systems can most usefully be adopted but, in general, the following principles should apply:

(a) The first and most important step is the assessment of the situation by a ship's officer who is experienced in the work and is thoroughly familiar with the relevant hazards.

(b) The information given in the permit should be precise, detailed and accurate. It should state exactly the location and details of the work to be done, the nature and results of any preliminary tests undertaken, the measures undertaken to make the job safe and the safeguards that need to be taken during the operation.

(c) The permit should specify the period of its validity (which should not exceed 24 hours) and any time limits applicable to the work which it authorises.

(d) The permit should be recognised as an overriding instruction until it is cancelled.

(e) Only the work specified on the permit should be undertaken.

(f) Before signing the permit, the responsible officer should personally check that all the measures specified as necessary have in fact been taken and that safety arrangements will be maintained until the permit is cancelled.

(g) Anyone who takes over, either as a matter of routine or in an emergency, from the person who originally issued the permit, should assume full responsibility until he has either cancelled the permit or handed it over to another nominated person who should be made fully conversant with the situation.

(h) The person responsible for carrying out the specified work should countersign the permit to indicate his understanding of the safety precautions to be observed. On completion of the work, he should notify the authorising officer.

4 The schedule at the end of this Chapter is a specimen form for a permit-to-work showing the headings that may need to be covered. It can be readily adapted to the exact circumstances of the job to be carried out, by amending wording, by deleting sections not relevant or by other changes which may be suitable.

5 In many instances a full permit-to-work system would be over-elaborate but there may still be a need to ensure that certain precautions are taken at appropriate stages of the work for the safety of those involved in the work or of those who may be

Specimen of a permit-to-work

SCHEDULE 1

Note: The Authorising Officer should indicate the sections applicable by ticks in the left-hand boxes next to headings, deleting any sub-heading not applicable. He should insert the appropriate details when the sections for *Other work* or *Additional precautions* are used.

The Authorised Person should tick each applicable right-hand box as he makes his check.

Work to be done (description)
Authorised person in charge
Period of validity of permit (should not exceed 24 hours)
Authorising Officer
(signed) (time) (date)

Location (designation of space, machinery, etc)

Crew detailed (names)

☐ **Entry into enclosed or confined spaces**

		checked
1	Space thoroughly ventilated	☐
2	Atmosphere tested and found safe	☐
3	Rescue and resuscitation equipment available at entrance	☐
4	Responsible person in attendance at entrance	☐
5	Communication arrangements made between person at entrance and those entering	☐
6	Access and illumination adequate	☐
7	All equipment to be used is of approved type	☐
8	When breathing apparatus is to be used	
	(i) Familiarity of user with apparatus is confirmed	☐
	(ii) Apparatus has been tested and found to be satisfactory.	☐

☐ **Machinery or equipment**

		checked
1	Removed from service/isolated from sources of power or heat	☐
2	All relevant personnel informed	☐

☐ **Hot work**	checked
1 Area clear of dangerous material and gas-free	☐
2 Ventilation adequate	☐
3 Equipment in good order	☐
4 Fire appliances in good order	☐

☐ **Other work**	checked
1	☐
2	☐
3	☐
4	☐

☐ **Additional precautions**	checked
1	☐
2	☐
3	☐
4	☐

Certificate of checks

I am satisfied that all precautions have been taken and that safety arrangements will be maintained for the duration of the work.

Authorised person in charge (signed)

Certificate of completion

The work has been completed and all persons under my supervision, materials and equipment have been withdrawn.

Authorised person in charge (signed) (time) (date)

affected by it. A rather simpler check list can be a useful aid in such cases. For example it could cover the posting of warning notices and the isolation of controls where the actuation of machinery or equipment could imperil men working at a place remote from the control position, especially aloft and overside, work on alarm and automatic systems and entry into refrigerated spaces.

CHAPTER 8

Accommodation ladders, gangways and other means of access

1 General

1.1 Care should be taken at all times when boarding or leaving a ship. Members of the crew should use only the authorised means of access.

1.2 Care should be taken when moving through the dock area, particularly at night. The edges of the docks, quays etc should be avoided. Where there are designated routes they should be followed exactly and this is especially important when crossing container terminals or other areas where rail traffic, straddle carriers or other mechanical handling equipment is operating, since the operators of such equipment have restricted visibility and anyone walking within the working area is at serious risk.

2 Maintenance

2.1 Gangways, accommodation ladders and portable ladders and their associated fittings and equipment should be inspected before and during use. Any defects should be made good before further use.

2.2 Wooden accommodation ladders, gangways and portable ladders should not be painted nor treated in such a way as to conceal any cracks or defects.

2.3 Defects or inadequacies found in any access arrangements, including those provided by the dock authorities, should be reported immediately.

3 Operation

3.1 Wherever practicable, the means of access should be sited clear of the cargo working area but, where this would be impracticable, access should be supervised.

3.2 The means of access and approaches thereto should be effectively illuminated, kept free from obstruction and as far as is practicable clear of any substance likely to cause a person to slip. In slippery conditions, appropriate warning notices should be posted and the surfaces suitably treated.

3.3 At the point of access on board the vessel, a lifebuoy with a self-activating light and an attached line of adequate length should be kept ready for immediate use.

3.4 When the in-board end of the gangway or accommodation ladder rests on or is flush with the top of the bulwark, a suitable bulwark ladder should be provided, properly secured and adequately fenced. Any gap between the bulwark ladder and the gangway or accommodation ladder should be adequately fenced to a height of 1 metre.

3.5 Gangways etc should not be rigged on ships' rails unless the rail has been reinforced for this purpose.

3.6 Where the means of access is provided from the ship, it should be adequately supervised to ensure that adjustments are made when necessary due to tidal movements or change of trim and freeboard. Guard ropes and chains etc should be kept taut at all times.

3.7 The angle of inclination of the gangway or accommodation ladder should be kept within such limits as are specified. Gangways should not be used at a greater angle of inclination than 30 degrees from the horizontal unless specifically designed for greater angles. Accommodation ladders should not normally be used at an angle greater than 55 degrees below the horizontal.

3.8 If the gangway or accommodation ladder has fixed steps and the angle is such that personnel would have to walk on the edges of steps, suitable cleated duckboards should be laid over and secured to the gangway or ladder.

4 Portable ladders

4.1 A portable ladder should only be used for access to the ship where circumstances preclude the use of a gangway or accommodation ladder. The ladder should be of sound material, good design and construction, of adequate strength for the purpose intended and free from defects (see also Chapter 15, section 5).

4.2 A portable ladder should extend at least 1 metre above the upper landing place unless there are other suitable handholds. It should be properly secured against slipping or shifting sideways and be so placed as to afford a clearance of at least 150 mm behind the rungs.

4.3 When the ladder is resting against bulwarks or rails, suitable safe access to the deck, as recommended in 3.4, should be provided.

5 Rope ladders

5.1 A rope ladder should not generally be used as a means of access, except to or from vessels alongside one another in such circumstances that the use of any other means of access would be impracticable.

5.2 The rope ladder should be of adequate width and length and so constructed that it can be efficiently secured to the ship. The steps should give a foothold of not less than 115 mm in depth over a width of at least 400 mm. The steps should be equally spaced at intervals of 310 mm ($\pm$ 5 mm).

5.3 A ladder of more than 1.5 metres in length should be fitted with spreaders to prevent twisting.

5.4 The steps of a rope ladder should be so secured that they cannot turn over or tilt.

5.5 The rope ladder should be left in such a way that it either hangs fully extended from its securing point or is pulled up completely. It should not be left in such a way that any slack would suddenly pay out when the ladder is used.

5.6 The rope ladder should be inspected before it is rigged to make sure that it is in a good, safe condition and that there are no broken or faulty steps.

5.7 The ladder should never be secured to rails unless the rails are so constructed and fixed as to take the weight of man and ladder with an ample margin of safety.

6 Safety nets

6.1 A safety net of suitable design should, where necessary and practicable, be spread below the means of access to arrest the fall of anyone slipping.

7 Special circumstances

7.1 In some circumstances (for example, the frequent movement of bulk carriers is sometimes necessary during loading to facilitate trimming of the cargo and also because of the nature of the loading operation itself), it may not at all times be practicable to mount a proper and safe means of access by conventional means. On such occasions, access to the vessel should be specially supervised or consideration given to providing alternative means of access, for example, by using the accommodation ladder on the offshore side of the vessel from which a suitable boat may operate to give access to a safe place on the quay.

7.2 Small boats or tender used to provide access between the shore and a ship moored away from the quay or jetty, should be safe and stable, be suitably powered, provide adequate protection against the weather and be properly equipped with the necessary safety equipment. They should not be used in unsuitable sea conditions.

CHAPTER 9

Movement about the ship

1 General

1.1 Seamen readily adjust themselves to the movement of a ship whilst at sea, but sometimes have no warning of an unusual lurch or heavy roll that may catch them off balance. They should be always alert to this possibility.

1.2 Suitable footwear should always be worn protecting toes against accidental stubbing, affording a good hold on deck and giving the support of firm soles for negotiating ladders.

1.3 Extra care is needed when negotiating ladders when wearing seaboots or gloves.

1.4 Head injuries may be caused by jumping over or stepping onto storm steps, sills, or other obstacles.

1.5 Rails are fitted to the side or overhead of stairs for steadying purposes and should not be used to swing on.

2 Passageways and walkways

2.1 Permanent fittings which may cause obstruction, such as eye plates on deck, lashing points and projections, should be painted a conspicuous colour in contrast to the background so that they are more easily seen. It may be useful to pad a sharp projection.

2.2 Any gear or equipment stowed to the side of a walkway or on the deck head should be securely lashed against the movement of the ship.

2.3 Wires and ropes should be coiled in a seamanlike fashion as close as practicable so as to cause least obstruction.

2.4 Sand or some other suitable substance should be spread over areas made slippery by snow, ice or rain. The utmost care must be taken in crossing such areas and particularly in using gangways, stairs and ladders under such conditions. Spillages of oil or grease etc should be cleaned up as soon as practicable.

2.5 When rough weather may be expected, lifelines should be rigged across open decks.

3 Watertight doors

3.1 Extra care is needed in using passageways closed by power-actuated watertight doors controlled from the bridge. The local control must be held continuously in the open position while any person is passing through the doorway, otherwise the door will close automatically with considerable force. Controls are arranged on each side of the bulkhead so that a person passing through may reach them simultaneously and keep them in the open position for the duration of his transit. A man by himself needs to use both hands and should therefore never attempt to carry any load through unassisted.

3.2 Notices clearly stating the method of operation of the local controls should be prominently displayed on both sides of each watertight door.

3.3 No one should attempt to pass through a watertight door when it is closing or the warning bell is sounding.

4 Lighting

4.1 Whenever possible, adequate lighting should be provided where men are moving about or working. This is most important on stairs and ladders. If it is necessary to enter or cross unlighted areas, the utmost care should be taken.

4.2 Artificial illumination should be reasonably uniform. Where possible, those passing from one area to another should not be subjected to contrasting levels of illumination. Broken or defective lights should be reported and repaired as soon as practicable.

4.3 Where portable lighting has to be used, fittings and leads etc should be suitable and safe for the intended usage. To avoid risks of electric shock from mains voltage, the portable lamps used in particularly damp or humid conditions should be of low voltage, preferably 12 volts.

4.4 Portable lights should never be lowered or suspended by their leads. The leads should be kept clear of running gear, moving parts of machinery, equipment and loads; if they pass through doorways, the doors should be secured open; they should be kept out of walkways as far as practicable to prevent people tripping over them. Any slack should be coiled.

4.5 Lights should not be switched off or removed without a check that all seamen are out of the space or area illuminated.

5 Guard rails round openings

5.1 Where openings through which a person may fall, or where a passage or access way, such as a catwalk, abuts a space into which a person may fall, are not adequately guarded by a permanent fencing arrangement or coamings at least to a clear height of 760 mm (30 inches), temporary guards or fencing should be fitted to a height of 1 metre (39 inches).

5.2 Guard rails or fencing should be of adequate strength, good construction, free from sharp edges and properly maintained.

5.3 Upper and lower rails and suitable stops or toeboards should be provided.

5.4 Where portable stanchions are used they should be secure against accidental displacement and fit firmly in a vertical position so as to ensure that each course of rails is kept substantially horizontal and taut throughout its length.

6 Fixed ladders and stairs

6.1 Fixed ladders, landings and cages etc should be inspected frequently and properly maintained. Those in holds should be examined for damage immediately after discharge of cargo.

6.2 Where a fixed ladder, handgrip or ladder cleat is found to be unsafe or when a ladder has been removed, for cargo handling for example, access should be blocked off. Repairs should be undertaken as soon as practicable but, until these have been effected or the ladder replaced, warning notices should be posted at each approach and alternative safe means of access provided.

6.3 Approaches to ladders and stairs should be at least 400 mm (16 inches) wide and unobstructed.

6.4 If a ladder does not reach 1 metre (39 inches) or more above the top landing place, suitable handholds or stanchions extending to that height should be provided.

6.5 Where the length of a vertical ladder or of a series of ladders in the same straight line exceeds 9 metres (30 feet) without a suitable landing platform, a harness or lifeline should be available for use by the person climbing the ladder, and should be worn by him where practicable.

6.6 Where access by fixed ladders or stairs is not practicable, portable rigid ladders may be used. They must be properly secured and have adequate clearance behind the rungs (see Chapter 15, section 5). Rope ladders should not be used for the purpose.

7 Drainage

7.1 Lower decks which need to be washed down frequently or are liable to become wet and slippery, as in the galley or ship's laundry, should be provided with effective means for draining off the water.

7.2 Where drainage is by way of channels in the deck, these should be suitably covered and the covers properly maintained.

7.3 Duckboards, where used, should be soundly constructed and designed so as to prevent accidental tripping. Regular examination of the boards should be carried out and any necessary repairs completed as soon as possible.

8 Ship's lifts

8.1 Ship's lifts should be provided with a telephone or with some other effective means of summoning assistance in an emergency.

CHAPTER 10

Entering enclosed or confined spaces

1 General

1.1 The atmosphere in any enclosed spaces not continuously or adequately ventilated, such as cargo or other tanks, cargo holds, pump rooms, cofferdams, duct keels and stores, may contain toxic or flammable gases or be deficient of oxygen to the extent of being incapable of supporting human life. Examples are:

(a) a space containing or having last contained combustible or flammable cargoes;

(b) a space containing, or having last contained, cargoes or stores of a toxic, corrosive, oxygen absorbing or irritant nature. Toxic gases may emanate from certain bulk cargoes. Residues from cleared bulk cargoes and leakages from packaged cargo offer similar risks;

(c) cargo spaces, ballast tanks or other spaces which have been inerted or fumigated;

(d) spaces wherein heating stoves, boilers, or internal combustion engines are installed;

(e) refrigerated cargo spaces in ships fitted with direct expansion plants, from which refrigerant may leak;

(f) spaces in which welding has taken place leaving residual fumes;

(g) spaces in which fires have occurred which consume oxygen and usually produce toxic combustion products;

(h) spaces immediately adjacent to the spaces referred to above, especially pumprooms and duct keels which may contain toxic fumes released from leakages of cargo, and including cofferdams and double bottom tanks around and beneath cargo spaces.

2 Lack of oxygen

2.1 If an empty tank has been left sealed for a time, the oxygen content of the atmosphere may be reduced due to oxygen combining with steel in the process of rusting. Lack of oxygen will also occur in a laid up boiler or other vessels where oxygen-absorbing chemicals have been used to reduce rusting. Depletion of oxygen may occur in holds when oxygen absorbing cargoes are carried, for example, vegetable products which have begun to rot or ferment, wood chips, steel products which have begun to rust, etc.

2.2 Hydrogen may occur in a cathodically-protected cargo tank used for ballast but will tend to disperse readily when tank covers are opened. Pockets of hydrogen may, however, still exist in the upper parts of the compartment, thus displacing the oxygen (as well as creating a possible explosion hazard).

2.3 If carbon dioxide or steam has been discharged, for example to extinguish or prevent a fire, the oxygen content will be reduced in the affected space.

2.4 The use of inert gas in the cargo tanks of tankers for permanently inerting those spaces, results in only minimal amounts of oxygen being present.

3 Testing for oxygen, gases and vapours

3.1 There are principally three types of instrument for testing the atmosphere in an enclosed space, the combustible gas indicator, the chemical absorption type of detector and the oxygen content meter.

3.2 The combustible gas indicator (or explosimeter) detects the presence and proportion of hydrocarbon vapour in air. It is not suitable for detecting gases and vapours at very low concentrations. It does not indicate oxygen deficiency or reliably indicate the presence of hydrogen, nor does it measure toxicity in the atmosphere.

3.3 Chemical absorption detectors are particularly useful for detecting the presence of specific gases and vapours at Threshold Limit Value levels. Threshold Limit Values (usually quoted for gases in parts per million – ppm) relate to daily exposure rates of 8 hours but these values of average tolerable concentration are a useful guide in the control of hazards in confined spaces. Amongst the substances whose presence may be accurately established by these detectors are benzene and hydrogen sulphide. Before using any test instrument, the manufacturer's instructions and advice on the limitations of the equipment should always be consulted and understood.

3.4 Oxygen testing equipment should be carried on all ships and should be used to measure the percentage of oxygen present within the space where it is suspected that there may be a deficiency.

4 Entering an enclosed or confined space

4.1 When it is necessary to enter an enclosed or confined space, the following principal points should be observed:

(a) identifying potential hazards;

(b) instituting and adhering to a rigid 'permit-to-work' system (see 4.2 below);

(c) ensuring that the space is secure against ingress of injurious substances;

(d) freeing the atmosphere of gas and removing sludge or other source of gas if necessary;

(e) testing for the presence of toxic gases and/or oxygen deficiency;

(f) instructing or training personnel in the safe conduct of the operation;

(g) providing adequate safety equipment;

(h) organising emergency rescue teams, first aid

Arranging regular drills will help to ensure that the necessary safety measures are consistently adopted.

4.2 The Master and responsible officers must be fully aware of any relevant hazards and the problems involved. Advance planning, preferably in the form of a 'permit-to-work' is necessary to evaluate the situation and ensure that all the necessary safety measures and precautions are taken (see Chapter 7). If, during the course of the operation, unforeseen difficulties or hazards develop, the work should be stopped if it is possible and practicable, so that the situation can be fully re-assessed. 'Permits-to-work' should be revised appropriately.

4.3 No person should enter an enclosed or confined space without the prior permission of the Master or a responsible officer, who should ensure that all necessary safety precautions are taken, as indicated in 4.1.

4.4 The space should be thoroughly ventilated by either natural or mechanical means before entry is made. Ventilation should continue during the period that the space is occupied and during temporary breaks, eg meal times. In the event of a failure of the ventilation system, any persons in the space should leave it immediately.

4.5 Where practicable, the testing of the atmosphere of the space before entry for oxygen deficiency and harmful gas or vapour should be carried out at different levels. Further tests should be made periodically at appropriate levels whilst the space is occupied so that requisite action may be taken if conditions worsen (see section 3).

4.6 Where the Master of officer in charge has doubts from the information available concerning the adequacy of ventilation or testing, breathing apparatus should be worn by those entering the space (see section 5).

4.7 In all cases rescue and, where available, resuscitation equipment should be ready for use at the entrance to the space.

4.8 A responsible person should be in constant attendance at the entrance to the space during the period that it is occupied.

4.9 An adequate system of communication should be agreed and tested by all involved to ensure that those entering the space can keep in touch with the person stationed at the entrance.

4.10 If a person in the space feels himself becoming in any way affected by vapours, he should give the pre-arranged signal to the person standing by at the entrance and immediately leave the space.

4.11 The officers on watch on the deck and in the engine room should be informed when any tank or compartment is to be entered.

4.12 Precautions should be taken to safeguard the continuity of any air supply required for breathing apparatus with special attention given to supplies originating from the engine room. Suitable warning notices should be posted at appropriate positions.

4.13 When an enclosed space is unattended, the entrance to it should where practicable be closed or fenced off. A notice should be posted prohibiting all unauthorised entry.

4.14 Access to and within the space should be adequate and well lit. No portable lights or other electrical equipment other than of an approved type should be taken or put into a compartment until it has been positively ascertained that it is safe to do so.

5 Entry into a space where the atmosphere is suspect or is known to be unsafe

5.1 No one should enter a space where it is known that the atmosphere is unsafe or will not support human life except when it is essential for the safety of life or of the ship. Breathing apparatus of an approved type should then be worn. RESPIRATORS PROVIDE NO PROTECTION IN SUCH CIRCUMSTANCES (see Chapter 5, section 5).

5.2 When breathing apparatus is being worn for working, two separate air supplies should be available to the wearer in case of a failure in one, except only where the urgency of rescue operations dictates otherwise. The practice of two or more persons wearing airline breathing apparatus all being connected to a single air supply should not be followed.

5.3 The apparatus should never be removed while the person is in the space.

5.4 All persons likely to be required to wear breathing apparatus should be completely familiar with the type of equipment to be used.

5.5 A person who is to enter the space should, before entry, make the following checks of his breathing apparatus together with the Master or officer in charge of the work operation:

(a) air supply pressure;

(b) audibility and operating pressure of low pressure alarm on self-contained breathing apparatus;

(c) leak-tightness of face-mask and adequacy of air supply (see Chapter 5, section 5).

5.6 Before entering any particular space, due regard should be paid to the difficulty of movement when wearing the available breathing apparatus and the problems which might be presented in the recovery of an incapacitated person in these circumstances.

6 Additional safety equipment

6.1 Lifelines and safety harnesses should be available and worn where practicable by all those entering tanks where either the atmosphere is suspect or known to be unsafe or where there is a risk of falling from a height. The lifeline should be capable of easy detachment by the wearer in case of entanglement.

6.2 Resuscitators of an appropriate kind are recommended for carriage on all ships but are essential equipment for:

(a) tankers carrying cargoes having a flash point below 60°C;

(b) ships carrying dangerous liquid chemicals in bulk, and ships carrying liquefied gases in bulk;

(c) other ships where entry into potentially hazardous enclosed spaces might be required.

7 Rescue

7.1 Any attempt to rescue a person who has collapsed within an enclosed space should be based on a pre-arranged plan having regard to the type of ship involved, the equipment on board and the manpower available. Drills should be held at regular intervals to prove the feasibility of the plan under different and difficult emergency conditions. Allocation of personnel to relieve or back up those first in action must always be borne in mind.

7.2 Pre-planning is essential if any success at all is to be achieved as survival after loss of air supply is time dependent and restoring the victim's oxygen requirements is the first priority. If the rescue operation is a long one, the continued supply of fully charged air cylinders for the self-contained breathing apparatus of the rescue team and/or the provision of a virtually inexhaustible air supply to those at the scene of the accident from a source of compressed air, is essential.

7.3 As enclosed spaces can range from the cavernous tanks of a VLCC to a low height double bottom tank with its cellular construction, every ship will have its own individual problems each of which may require a different rescue procedure. Notwithstanding this, many of the procedures are universally applicable as the following paragraph illustrates.

7.4 If there are indications through the agreed system of communication or otherwise of the person in the space being affected by the atmosphere, the person outside the space, referred to in para 4.8 should immediately raise the alarm informing the Master and officer in charge of the deck and/or engine room as circumstances permit. ON NO ACCOUNT SHOULD THE PERSON STATIONED AT THE ENTRANCE ATTEMPT TO ENTER THE SPACE BEFORE ADDITIONAL HELP HAS ARRIVED. If air is being supplied to the person in the space through an air line, a check that the supply is being maintained at the correct pressure should immediately be made. No rescue must be attempted without breathing apparatus and a lifeline. Every moment is vital but this should not influence the rescue team towards taking unnecessary risks. Unless the man is gravely injured, eg a broken back, any physical injury he has sustained is of secondary importance. The victim must be brought out with the least delay when his physical injuries can be attended to but it is emphasised that restoration of the casualty's air supply at the earliest possible moment must always be the first priority.

8 Maintenance of equipment

8.1 All breathing apparatus, safety harnesses, lifelines, resuscitation equipment and any other equipment provided for use in, or in connection with, entry into enclosed spaces, and for use in emergencies, must be properly maintained. All items of breathing apparatus should be examined periodically and as soon as possible after every occasion on which the apparatus has been used (see Chapter 5.

8.2 Atmospheric testing and sampling equipment, oxygen meters, explosimeters etc should also be regularly maintained and, where applicable, calibrated. Due regard should be paid to manufacturers' recommendations, which should always be kept with the equipment.

CHAPTER 11

Manual lifting and carrying

1 In manual lifting and carrying, the proper procedure to be followed as a matter of habit is to size up the load to be lifted, look for sharp edges, protruding nails or splinters, for greasy or other surfaces which may affect grip and for any other features which may prove awkward or dangerous; for example sacks of bulk commodities may be difficult to get off the deck.

2 The deck or area over which the load is to be moved, should be free from obstructions and not slippery.

3 A firm and balanced stance should be taken close to the load with feet a little apart, not too wide, so that the lift will be as straight as possible.

4 A crouching position should be adopted, knees bent and back straight to ensure that the legs do the work – keeping chin tucked in.

The right way
Legs bent, back straight, using the strong leg muscles to lift.

The wrong way
Legs straight, back bent— the back muscles being used at risk of injury to spine.

5 The load should be gripped with the whole of the hand – not fingers only. If there is insufficient room under a heavy load to do this a piece of wood should be put underneath first.

6 Size is not a good guide to weight and a trial lift should be made. If there is any doubt whether the load can be managed by one man, help should be provided.

7 When two or more men are handling a load, it is preferable that they should be of similar height. The actions of lifting, lowering and carrying should, as far as possible, be carried out in unison to prevent strain and any tendency for either person to overbalance.

8 The load should be lifted by straightening the legs, keeping it close to the body. The body should not be twisted as this will impose undue strain.

9 If the lift is to a high level, it may be necessary to do it in two stages; first raising the load on to a bench or other support and then completing the lift to the full height, with a fresh grip.

10 The procedure for putting a load down is the reverse of that for lifting, the legs should do the work of lowering – knees bent, back straight and the load close to the body. Care should be taken not to trap fingers. The load should not be put down in a position where it is unstable.

11 A load should always be carried in such a way that it does not obscure vision, so that any obstruction in the passageway can be seen.

12 Suitable shoes or boots should be worn for the job. Protective toecaps help to guard toes from crushing if the load slips; they can sometimes also be useful when putting the load down to take the weight while hands are removed from underneath.

13 Clothing should be worn which does not catch in the load and which gives some body protection.

14 Where the work is very strenuous, either because of the weight of the load or because of repetitive efforts over a period,

rest should be taken at suitable intervals, to allow muscles, heart and lungs to recover; fatigue makes accidents more likely on work of this kind.

CHAPTER 12

Tools and materials

1 Hand tools

1.1 A tool is designed for one particular function and no other. It should be treated with respect. The material of which it is made is appropriate to the intended purpose but usually not to others. Files are hard but brittle; screwdriver shanks bend where levers do not, and pliers may slip on nuts.

1.2 For every job, the proper tools in the right sizes should be available and used. Tools used for a purpose for which they were not designed may cause injury to the user and damage to the workpiece and the tools.

1.3 Damaged or worn tools should not be used. Handles of hammers, screwdrivers and chisels should be secure; wooden handles should be straight-grained, smooth and without splinters. Punches and cold chisels with jagged heads should not be used. Cutting edges should be kept sharp and clean. Faces of hammers, punches and spanners should be true. Repair and dressing of the tools should be carried out by a competent person.

1.4 When not in use, they should be stowed tidily in a suitable tool rack, box or carrier, with cutting edges protected.

1.5 Wherever practicable, a tool in use should be directed away from the body to avoid injury should the tool or workpiece slip.

1.6 Both hands should be kept behind the cutting edge of a wood chisel.

1.7 A cold chisel is best held between thumb and base of index finger with thumb and fingers straight, palm of hand facing towards the hammer blow.

1.8 A saw should not be forced, it should be pushed with a light, even movement.

2 Portable electric, pneumatic and hydraulic tools

2.1 Power-operated tools may be dangerous unless properly maintained, handled and used.

2.2 Because of the greatly increased risk of electric shock from supplies at mains voltage, portable electric equipment for use in particularly damp or humid conditions should be of extra low voltage pattern (not more than 50V AC with a maximum of 30V to earth, or 50V DC).

2.3 Double-insulated tools (where the exposed metal parts are not designed for earth connection) are not recommended for use on ships because water (which may be salt-laden) can provide a contact between live parts and the casing, increasing the risk of a fatal shock when the tool is used.

2.4 The power supply lead and connections should be inspected before a tool is used; defects should be repaired and the tool tested by a competent person before its re-use.

2.5 The flexible cables of electric tools should comply with the relevant British Standard and be provided with proper connections to the power supply. The tools should be properly earthed.

2.6 The fuse or circuit-breaker on the line of supply to electric power tools should be of the minimum rating practicable. This is most important if double-insulated tools are used.

2.7 Electric leads and the hoses of pneumatic and hydraulic tools should be kept clear of damage from nails, sharp edges, hot surfaces, oil and chemicals etc. Where leads or hoses pass through doorways or other openings, the doors etc should be secured open. Where they trail across decks or passageways, leads or hoses should wherever possible be suspended high enough to give clearance over men passing.

2.8 Whip-lash from pneumatic hoses in the event of breakage of couplings, may be prevented by fitting chain linkages between sections of the hose or alternatively incorporating safety valves which close off the lines.

2.9 Accessories or tool pieces should be absolutely secure in the tool. In particular, retaining springs, clamps, locking levers and other built-in safety devices on pneumatic tools should be replaced after the toolpiece (drill, bit, chisel etc) is changed. Serious injuries can be caused if any of these are omitted, since the tool-piece may be ejected with considerable force when power is applied.

2.10 Accessories or fitments should not be fixed or replaced while the tool is connected to a source of power.

2.13 Where a safety guard is needed for a particular operation, it should be securely fixed before work begins; if it is removed for changing an accessory, it should be replaced immediately.

2.14 During a temporary interruption of work, power tools should be switched off and disconnected from the source of power and left in a safe position with leads clear of passageways. A check that the switch or control is off should always be made before the tool is reconnected.

2.15 Where the work operation causes high noise levels, hearing protection should be worn. Where flying particles may be produced, the face and eyes should be protected (see Chapter 5).

2.16 The vibration caused by reciprocating tools (pneumatic drills, hammers, chisels etc) or high-speed rotating tools (eg drills) can give rise to a disablement of the hands known as 'dead' or 'white' fingers. In its initial stages, this appears as a numbness of the fingers and an increasing sensitivity to cold but in more advanced stages, the hands become blue and the finger-tips swollen. Men prone to the disability should not use such portable power tools.

3 Workshop and bench machines (fixed installations)

3.1 No one should operate a machine unless authorised to do so. The operator should be competent in its use and familiar with its controls. He should not attempt to use it if he has bandaged hands. (See Chapter 1, section 3 about garments, long hair etc.)

3.2 All dangerous parts of machines should be provided with efficient guards which should be properly secured before the machine is put into operation. Self-adjusting guards are preferable where the position of the guard has to relate to the workpiece. Grinding machines should be fitted with eye screens which need to be renewed from time-to-time.

3.3 Guards should be made preferably in solid material. Where they are of perforated metal, mesh or bars, the openings should not be large enough to allow a finger to be inserted to reach a dangerous part.

3.4 Controls of machines and switches for supplementary lighting, where this is provided, should not be so placed that the operator has to lean over the machine to reach them.

3.5 A machine should be checked every time before use. It should not be operated when a guard or safety device is missing, incorrectly adjusted or defective or when it is itself in any way faulty.

3.6 If defective in any respect, the machine should be isolated from its source of power pending adjustment or repair. Only a competent person should attempt repairs. Unskilled interference with electrical equipment in particular is highly dangerous.

3.7 Work benches should be well lit and some machines may require individual supplementary lights.

3.8 Working areas should be kept uncluttered and, as far as practicable, free of litter and spilled oil. Loose gear, tools and equipment not required for immediate use should be cleared away and properly stowed.

3.9 Swarf (metal turnings, filings and the like) should not be allowed to pile up round a machine. The machine should be stopped for its removal. A rake or similar device should be used for the purpose, never the bare hand.

3.10 A heavy item of equipment brought into a workshop for repair should be made secure against accidental movement.

3.11 Appropriate eye and face protection should be worn during chipping, scaling, wirebrushing, grinding and similar work where particles may fly; this is a special risk in turning brass (see Chapter 5).

3.12 Where sanding or other processes generate a lot of dust in the air, dust masks or respirators should be worn (see Chapter 5).

3.13 Other people working in the area may need the protection indicated in either of the two preceding paragraphs.

3.14 Before a lathe or drill is started, the chuck key should be removed and the operator should make sure that other people are clear of the machine.

3.15 A machine should be stopped when not in use, even if it is expected to be left unattended for a few moments only. The machine should be rechecked on every occasion before being started up again in case controls, guards etc have been altered or moved while the machine has been left unattended.

3.16 Where a machine is driven by a V-belt in conjunction with a stepped pulley, and alterations in spindle speed require a change in the belt position, means should be provided if practicable for the belt tension to be eased during that operation; the position of the belt should never be changed while the machine is running.

3.17 Work pieces for drilling or milling should be at all times securely held by a machine vice or clamp.

3.18 Material projecting beyond the headstock of a lathe should be securely fenced.

4 Abrasive wheels

4.1 Abrasive wheels should be selected, mounted and used only by competent persons and in accordance with manufacturers' instructions.

4.2 Abrasive wheels are relatively fragile and should be stored and handled with care.

4.3 Manufacturers' instructions should be followed on the selection of the correct type of wheel for the job in hand. Generally, soft wheels are more suitable for hard material and hard wheels for soft material.

4.4 Before a wheel is mounted, it should be brushed clean and closely inspected to ensure that it has not been damaged in storage or transit. The soundness of a vitrified wheel can be further checked by suspending it vertically and tapping it gently. If the wheel sounds dead it is probably cracked, and should not be used.

4.5 A wheel should not be mounted on a machine for which it is unsuitable.

4.6 The wheel should fit freely but not loosely on the spindle; if the fit is unduly tight, the wheel may crack as the heat of operation causes the spindle to expand.

4.7 The clamping nut should be tightened only sufficiently to hold the wheel firmly. When the flanges are clamped by a series of screws, the screws should be first screwed home with the fingers and diametrically opposite pairs tightened in sequence.

4.8 The speed of the spindle should not exceed the stated maximum permissible speed for the wheel.

4.9 A strong guard should be provided and kept in position at every abrasive wheel (unless the nature of the work absolutely precludes its use) both to contain wheel parts in the event of a burst and to prevent an operator having contact with the wheel.

4.10 The guard should enclose as much of the wheel as possible.

4.11 Where a workrest is provided, it should be properly secured to the machine and should be adjusted as close as practicable to the wheel, the gap normally being not more than 1.5 mm ($\frac{1}{16}$ inch).

4.12 The side of a wheel should not be used for grinding: it is particularly dangerous when the wheel is appreciably worn.

4.13 The workpiece should never be held in a cloth or pliers.

4.14 When dry grinding operations are being carried on or when an abrasive wheel is being trued or dressed, suitable transparent screens should be fitted in front of the exposed part of the wheel or operators should wear properly fitting eye protectors.

5 Spirit lamps

5.1 Care should be taken in filling spirit lamps. Fuel should not be added to a lamp which has been in use until it has completely cooled down.

6 Compressed air

6.1 When compressed air is used, the pressure should be kept no higher than is necessary to undertake the work satisfactorily.

6.2 Compressed air should not be used to clean the working space.

6.3 In no circumstances should compressed air be directed at any part of a person's body.

7 Compressed gas cylinders

7.1 Compressed gas cylinders should always be handled with care, whether full or empty. They should be properly secured and kept upright. If available, cylinder trolleys should be used to transport cylinders from one place to another.

7.2 The protective caps over the valve should be screwed in place when the cylinders are not in use or are being moved. Valves should be closed when the cylinder is empty.

7.3 Empty cylinders should be segregated from full ones and/or be so marked. Cylinders should be stored in a place where they will not be subject to extremes in temperature.

7.4 Special precautions as follows need to be taken in the case of cylinders of oxygen and acetylene or other fuel gases:

(a) cylinder valves, controls and associated fittings should be kept free from oil, grease and paint. Controls should not be operated with oily hands;

(b) gas should not be taken from such cylinders unless the correct pressure reducing regulator has been attached to the cylinder outlet valve;

(c) cylinders found to have leaks that cannot be stopped by closing the outlet valve should be taken to the open deck away from any sources of heat or ignition and slowly discharged to the atmosphere.

7.5 Identifying markings on cylinders are set out in Chapter 6, section 5.

8 Chemical agents

8.1 A chemical from an unlabelled container should never be used unless its identity has been positively established.

8.2 Chemicals should always be handled with the utmost care. Eyes and skin should be protected from accidental exposure or contact.

8.3 Manufacturers' or suppliers advice on the correct use of the chemicals should always be followed. Some cleaning agents, even though used domestically, for example, caustic soda and bleaches, may burn the skin.

8.4 Chemicals should not be mixed unless it is known that dangerous reactions will not be caused.

CHAPTER 13

Welding and flamecutting operations

1 General

1.1 Welding and flamecutting elsewhere than in the workshop should generally be the subject of a 'permit-to-work' (see Chapter 7).

1.2 Operators should be competent in the process, familiar with the equipment to be used and instructed where special precautions need to be taken.

1.3 Where portable lights are needed to provide adequate illumination, they should be clamped or otherwise secured in position, not hand-held, with leads kept clear of the working area.

1.4 Harmful fumes can be produced during these operations especially from galvanising, paint, etc. Oxygen in the atmosphere can be depleted when using gas cutting equipment and noxious gases may be produced when welding or cutting. Special care should therefore be taken when welding and flamecutting in enclosed spaces to provide adequate ventilation. The effectiveness of the ventilation should be checked at intervals while the work is in progress. In confined spaces, breathing apparatus may be required.

1.5 Welding and flamecutting equipment should be inspected before use by a competent person to ensure that it is in a serviceable condition. All repairs should be carried out by a competent person.

2 Protective clothing

2.1 Protective clothing and equipment complying with the relevant British Standard Specifications should be worn by the operator and as appropriate by those working with him to protect them from particles of hot metal and slag and from accidental burns and their eyes and skin from ultra-violet and heat radiation.

2.2 The operator should normally wear:

(a) welding helmet with suitably coloured transparent eye piece. Eye goggles or a hand-held shield may be suitable alternatives in appropriate circumstances;

(b) leather working gloves;

(c) leather apron (in appropriate circumstances);

(d) long-sleeved natural fibre boiler suit or other approved protective clothing.

2.3 Clothing should be free of grease and oil and other flammable substances.

3 Precautions against fire

3.1 Before welding, flamecutting or other hot work is begun, a check should be made that there are no combustible solids, liquids or gases, at, below or adjacent to the area of the work, which might be ignited by heat or sparks from the work.

3.2 Welding or other hot work should never be undertaken on surfaces covered with grease, oil or other flammable or combustible substances.

3.3 When welding is to be done in the vicinity of open hatches, suitable screens should be erected to prevent sparks dropping down hatchways or hold ventilators. Where necessary, combustible materials and dunnage should be moved to a safe distance before commencing operations.

3.4 Port holes and other openings through which sparks may fall should be closed where practicable.

3.5 Where work is being done close to or at bulkheads, decks or deckheads, the remote sides of the divisions should be checked for materials and substances which may ignite, and for cables, pipelines or other services which may be affected by the heat.

3.6 Oil tanks etc should be certified free of flammable gases before any repair work is begun on them.

3.7 Suitable fire extinguishers should be kept at hand ready for use during the operation. A person with a suitable extinguisher should also be stationed to keep watch on areas not visible to the welder which may be affected.

3.8 In view of the risk of delayed fires resulting from the use of burning or welding apparatus, appropriate frequent checks should be made for at least two hours after cessation of the work.

4 Electric welding equipment

4.1 Electric welding sets for shipboard use should operate on direct current supply.

4.2 Where the direct current is obtained from rectified alternating current or where an alternating current set has to be employed, a voltage reduction device should be used to limit the idling voltage (before an arc is struck between electrode and workpiece) to 42 volts or 25 volts respectively. The proper functioning of the device (which may be affected by dust or humidity) should be checked each time the set is used.

4.3 A 'go and return' system utilising two cables from the welding set should be adopted; the welding return cable should be firmly clamped to the workpiece.

4.4 The welding set and the workpiece or workpieces should be separately earthed to the ship's structure. The use of a single cable with hull return is not recommended.

4.5 To avoid voltage drop in transmission, the lead and return cables should be of the minimum length practicable for the job and of an appropriate cross-section.

4.6 Cables should be inspected before use; if the insulation is impaired or conductivity is reduced, they should not be used.

4.7 Any cable connectors should be fully insulated and so designed and installed that live terminals are not exposed on disconnection.

4.8 Electrode holders should be fully insulated so that no live part of the holder is exposed to touch, and, where practicable, should be fitted with guards to prevent accidental contact with live electrodes and as protection from sparks and splashes of weld metal.

4.9 A local switching arrangement or other suitable means should be provided for rapid cutting off current from the electrode should the operator get into difficulties and also for isolating the holder when electrodes are changed.

5 Precautions to be taken during electric-arc welding

5.1 The welding operator should wear the protective clothing specified in 2.2 but should additionally wear non-conducting safety footwear. Clothing should be kept as dry as possible as some protection against electric shock; it is particularly important that gloves should be dry because wet leather is a good conductor.

5.2 An assistant should be in continuous attendance during welding operations. He should be alert to the risk of accidental shock to the welder, ready to cut off power instantly, raise the alarm and apply artificial respiration without delay. The desirability of a second assistant should be considered if the work is to be carried out in difficult conditions.

5.3 Where persons other than the operator are likely to be exposed to harmful radiation or sparks from electric arc welding, they should be protected by screens or other effective means.

5.4 In restricted spaces, where the operator may be in close contact with the ship's structure or is likely to make contact in the course of ordinary movements, protection should be provided by dry insulating mats or boards.

5.5 There are increased risks of electric shock to the operator if welding is done in hot or humid conditions; body sweat and damp clothing greatly reduce body resistance. Under such conditions, the operation should be deferred until such time as an adequate level of safety can be achieved.

5.6 In no circumstances should a welder work while standing in water or with any part of his body immersed.

5.7 The flux coating of an electrode is not always an insulator. The electrode holder should be isolated from current supply before a used electrode is removed, and before a new electrode is inserted.

5.8 When the welding operation is completed or temporarily suspended, the electrode should be removed from the holder.

5.9 Hot electrode ends should be ejected into a suitable container; they should not be handled with bare hands.

5.10 Spare electrodes should be kept dry in their box until required for use.

6 Gas welding and cutting

6.1 Advice on the storage and handling of gas cylinders is given in Chapter 12, section 7.

6.2 The pressure of oxygen used for welding should always be high enough to prevent acetylene flowing back into the oxygen line.

6.3 Acetylene should not be used for welding at a pressure exceeding 1 atmosphere gauge as it is liable to explode, even in the absence of air, when under excessive pressure.

6.4 An efficient back pressure valve and flame arrestor should be provided in the acetylene and oxygen supply lines as near as practicable to the burner.

6.5 Should an acetylene cylinder become hot as a result of a backfire through the use of faulty equipment, it should immediately be removed to the open deck and kept cool either by immersion or with copious amounts of water and the cylinder stop valve opened fully. If this cannot be done with safety, consideration should be given to jettisoning the cylinder overboard.

6.6 When acetylene cylinders are coupled together, flash arrestors should be used between the cylinders and the coupler block, or between the coupler block and the regulator.

6.7 Only acetylene cylinders of approximately equal pressures should be coupled.

6.8 In fixed installations, manifolds should be clearly marked with the gas they contain.

6.9 Manifold hose connections including inlet and outlet connections should be such that the hose cannot be interchanged between fuel gases and oxygen manifolds and headers.

6.10 Only those hoses specially designed for welding and cutting operations should be used to connect an oxy-acetylene blowpipe to gas outlets.

6.11 Any length of hose in which a flashback has occurred should be discarded.

6.12 The connections between hose and blowpipe and between hoses, should be securely fixed with metal fittings such as hose bands.

6.13 Hoses should be so arranged that they are not likely to become kinked or tangled or be tripped over, cut or otherwise damaged by moving objects or falling metal slag, sparks etc; a sudden jerk or pull on the hose is liable to pull the blowpipe out of the operator's hands or cause a cylinder to fall or a hose connection to fail. Hoses in passageways should be covered to avoid them becoming a tripping hazard.

6.14 Soapy water only should be used for testing leaks in hoses.

6.15 Blowpipes should be lit with a special friction igniter, stationary pilot flame or other safe means.

6.16 Should a blowpipe-tip opening become clogged, it should be cleaned only with the tools especially designed for that purpose.

6.17 When a blowpipe is to be changed the gases should be shut off at the pressure-reducing regulators.

6.18 During a temporary stoppage or after completion of the work, supply valves on gas cylinders and gas mains should be securely closed and blowpipes, hoses and moveable pipes should be removed to lockers that open on to the open deck, to prevent a build-up of dangerous concentrations of gas or fumes.

6.19 Oxygen should never be used to ventilate, cool or blow dust off clothing (see also Chapter 12, section 6).

CHAPTER 14

Painting

1 General

1.1 Paints may contain toxic or irritant substances, and the solvents may give rise to flammable and potentially explosive vapours, which may also be toxic; men using such paints should be warned of the particular risks arising from their use. Paints containing organic pesticides can be particularly dangerous. If the manufacturer's instructions are not given on the container, it should be ascertained at the time of supply whether any special hazards may arise from the use of the paint and also whether special methods of application should be followed. Such advice should be readily available at the time of use but the following precautions should always be taken in any case.

1.2 Painted surfaces should not be rubbed down dry unless it is known that the old paint is free from lead or other substance, the dust from which could be toxic if inhaled. Dust masks should be worn as protection against other dusts.

1.3 Rust removers are acids and contact with the skin should be avoided. Eye protection should be worn against splashes. If painting aloft or otherwise near ropes, care should be taken to avoid splashes on ropes, safety harness, lines, etc. Reference should be made to Chapter 15, section 4 on the effect of such contamination on ropes.

1.4 Interior and enclosed spaces should be well ventilated, both while painting is in progress and until the paint has dried.

1.5 There should be no smoking or use of naked lights in interior spaces during painting or until the paint has dried hard. Some vapours even in low concentrations may decompose into more harmful substances when passing through burning tobacco.

1.6 When painting is done in the vicinity of machinery, especially in the engine room or, for instance, from an overhead crane gantry, care should be taken to ensure that the power supply is isolated and the machinery immobilised in such a way that it cannot be moved or started up inadvertently. Appropriate warning notices should be posted (see Chapter 22, section 1.11). Close-fitting clothing should be worn (see Chapter 1, section 3).

2 Spraying

2.1 There are many different types of paint spraying equipment in use and operators should acquaint themselves with the manufacturer's instructions on the correct usage of the equipment prior to the operation, and how to avoid risks in use.

2.2 Airless spray painting equipment is particularly hazardous since the paint is ejected at very high pressure and can penetrate the skin or cause serious eye injuries to the operator or anyone else at close range. Great care should therefore be taken when this system is used.

2.3 Suitable protective clothing such as a combination suit, gloves, cloth hood, and eye protection should be worn during spraying.

2.4 Paints containing lead, mercury or similarly toxic compounds should not be sprayed in interiors.

2.5 A suitable respirator should be worn according to the nature of the paint being sprayed. In exceptional circumstances it may be necessary to use breathing apparatus (see Chapter 5, section 5).

2.6 If a spray nozzle clogs, the trigger of the gun should be locked in a closed position before any attempt is made to clear the blockage.

2.7 Before a blocked spray nozzle is removed or any other dismantling attempted, pressure should be relieved from the system.

2.8 A gun having a reversible nozzle calls for special care to ensure that hands are clear of the nozzle's orifice when a blockage is being removed by blowing through.

2.9 The pressure in the system should not exceed the recommended working pressure of the hose. The system should be regularly inspected for defects.

2.10 As an additional precaution against the hazards of a hose bursting, a loose sleeve, for example a length of 2 to 3 metres (6 to 10 feet) of old air hose, may be slipped over that portion of the line adjacent to gun and paint container.

3 Painting aloft, overside and from punts

3.1 The same precautions should be taken in painting aloft as for other work aloft (see Chapter 15).

3.2 Painting punts should be stable and provided with suitable fencing. Unsecured trestles and planks should not be used to give additional height.

3.3 The person in charge should have due regard to the strength of tides and other hazards, such as wash from passing vessels, before a painting punt is put to use.

3.4 A man painting overside should wear a life-line and buoyancy garment and should be under observation by a seaman on deck; a lifebuoy with a sufficient length of line attached should be ready for immediate use.

3.5 When painting is to be done at or near the stern or other propeller aperture, the person in charge should inform the duty engineer and deck officers so that warning notices are put up in the engine room, at the controls and on the bridge.

3.6 The duty engineer and deck officers should also be informed by the person in charge when seamen are painting below ship's side discharges so that they are not used until the work is completed. Notices to this effect should be attached to the relevant control valves and not taken off until the men are reported clear.

CHAPTER 15

Working aloft and outboard

1 General

1.1 A man working at a height may not be able to give his full attention to the job and at the same time guard himself against falling. Proper precautions should therefore always be taken to ensure personal safety when work has to be done aloft or when working outboard. It must be remembered that the movement of a ship in a seaway will add to the hazards involved in work of this type. A stage or ladder should always be utilised when work is to be done beyond normal reach.

1.2 Seamen under 18 years of age or with less than 12 months experience at sea, should not work aloft unless accompanied by an experienced seaman or otherwise adequately supervised.

1.3 A safety harness with lifeline or other arresting device should be continuously worn when working aloft, outboard or overside (see Chapter 5, section 7). A safety net should be rigged where necessary and appropriate. Additionally, where work is done overside, buoyancy garments should be worn and a lifebuoy with sufficient line attached should be kept ready for immediate use.

1.4 Men should not work overside while the vessel is under way.

1.5 Before work is commenced near the ship's whistle, the officer responsible for the job should ensure that power is shut off and warning notices posted on the bridge and in the machinery spaces.

1.6 Before work is commenced on the funnel, the officer responsible should inform the duty engineer to ensure that steps are taken to reduce as far as practicable the emission of steam, harmful gases and fumes.

1.7 Before work is commenced in the vicinity of radio aerials, the officer responsible should inform the radio officer so that no transmissions are made whilst there is risk to the seafarer. A warning notice should be put up in the radio room.

1.8 Where work is to be done near the radar scanner, the officer responsible should inform the officer on watch so that the radar and scanner are isolated. A warning notice should be put on the set until the necessary work has been completed.

1.9 On completion of the work of the type described above, the officer responsible should, where necessary, inform the appropriate officer that the precautions taken are no longer required and that warning notices can be removed.

1.10 Unless it is essential, work should not be done aloft on a stage or bosun's chair in the vicinity of cargo working.

1.11 Care must also be taken while work is being done aloft or at a height, to avoid risks to anyone working or moving below. Suitable warning notices should be displayed. Tools and stores should be sent up and lowered by line in suitable containers which should be secured in place for stowage of tools or materials not presently being used.

1.12 A tool should not be placed where it can be accidentally knocked off to fall on someone below, nor should tools be carried in pockets from which they may easily fall. A belt designed to hold much-used tools securely in loops will be found a great convenience.

1.13 Tools should be handled with extra care when hands are cold or greasy and where the tools themselves are greasy.

2 Cradles and stages

2.1 Cradles should be at least 430 mm (17 inches) wide and fitted with guard rails or stanchions with taut ropes to a height of 1 metre (39 inches) from the floor. Toeboards add safety.

2.2 Planks and materials used for the construction of ordinary plank stages must be carefully examined to ensure adequate strength and freedom from defect.

2.3 Wooden components of staging should be stowed in a dry, ventilated space and not subjected to heat.

2.4 Ancillary equipment, lizards, blocks and gantlines should be thoroughly examined before use. A defective item should not be used.

2.5 When a stage is rigged overside, the two gantlines used in its rigging should at least be long enough to trail into the water to provide additional lifelines should the operator fall. A lifebuoy and line should still be kept ready at a close position.

2.6 Gantlines should be kept clear of sharp edges.

2.7 The anchoring points for lines, blocks and lizards must be of adequate strength and, where practicable, be permanent fixtures to the ship's structure. Integral lugs should be hammer tested. Portable rails or stanchions should not be used as anchoring points. Beam clamps and similar devices should be used solely for their intended purposes and then only under close supervision.

2.8 Stages and staging which are not suspended should always be secured against movement. Hanging stages should be restricted against movement to the extent practicable.

2.9 In machinery spaces, staging and its supports should be kept clear of contact with hot surfaces and moving parts of machinery. In the engine room, a crane gantry should not be used directly as a platform for cleaning or painting, but can be used as the base for a stable platform if the precautions of Chapter 14, section 1.6 are taken.

2.10 Where men working from a stage are required to raise or lower themselves, great care must be taken to keep movements of the stage small and closely controlled.

3 Bosun's chairs

3.1 When used with a gantline the chair should be secured to it with a double sheet bend and the end seized to the standing part with adequate tail.

3.2 Hooks should not be used to secure bosun's chairs unless they are of the type which because of their special construction cannot be accidentally dislodged.

3.3 On each occasion that a bosun's chair is rigged for use, the chair, gantlines and lizards should be thoroughly examined, and a load test applied before a man is hoisted.

3.4 When a chair is to be used for riding topping lifts or stays, it is essential that the bow of the shackle, and not the pin, rides on the wire. The pin in any case should be seized.

3.5 When it is necessary to haul a seaman aloft in a bosun's chair it should be done only by hand; a winch should not be used.

3.6 If a man is required to lower himself while using a bosun's chair, he should first frap both parts of the gantline together with a suitable piece of line to secure the chair before making the lowering hitch. The practice of holding on with one hand and making the lowering hitch with the other is dangerous.

4 Ropes

4.1 The safety of the man aloft or overside depends upon the strength of the line holding him, whether it is a lifeline to his harness or gantline to a bosun's chair or stage.

4.2 Many types of rope of both man-made and natural fibre are available, each with different properties and with different resistance to contamination by substances in use about the ship which may seriously weaken the rope. Guidance on the selection of man-made fibre ropes can be found in the relevant British Standard (see Appendix 1). Seafarers should therefore be aware of the general limitations of the different types of rope and the following table is set out as a guide on the resistance of the main rope types to chemical attack.

This table is indicative only of the possible extent of deterioration of rope; in practice, much depends upon the precise formulation of the material, the amount of contamination the rope receives and the length of time and the temperature at which it is exposed to the contamination. In some cases, damage may not be apparent even on close visual inspection.

	Resistance to chemicals of rope made of			
Substance	Manila or Sisal	Polyamide (nylon)	Polyester	Polypropylene
Sulphuric (battery) acid	None	Poor	Good	V Good
Hydrochloric acid	None	Poor	Good	V Good
Typical rust remover	Poor	Fair	Good	V Good
Caustic soda	None	Good	Fair	V Good
Liquid bleach	None	Good	V Good	V Good
Creosote, crude oil	Fair	None	Good	V Good
Phenols, Crude tar	Good	Fair	Good	Good
Diesel oil	Good	Good	Good	Good
Synthetic detergents	Poor	Good	Good	Good
Chlorinated solvents, eg trichloroethylene (used in some paint and varnish removers)	Poor	Fair	Good	Poor
Other organic solvents	Good	Good	Good	Good

4.3 Ropes should be stored away from heat and sunlight, and in a separate compartment from containers of chemicals, detergents, rust removers, paint strippers or other substances capable of damaging them.

4.4 The person responsible for the work being undertaken should ensure that all ropes, lifelines, gantlines etc employed for a particular job are resistant to attack by substances that might be used during the course of that job. Ropes of natural fibres, or a mixture of natural and man-made fibres, should not be used for these purposes. Similarly, care should be taken in the selection and use of ancillary equipment such as safety harnesses and safety nets.

4.5 Polypropylene ropes which have the best all round resistance to attack by harmful substances are generally preferred but unless they are of a type resistant to actinic degradation, such as those approved for life-saving appliances by the Department of Trade, they should not be exposed to strong sunlight for long periods. They should also be of a type providing grip comparable to that of manila or sisal ropes.

4.6 Rope of man-made material stretches under load to an extent which varies according to the material. Polyamide rope stretches the most.

4.7 Rope should be inspected internally and externally before use for signs of deterioration, undue wear or damage. This is particularly important if a gantline has not been used for some time. A high degree of powdering between strands of man-made fibre ropes indicates hard wear and impaired strength: the internal wear will be greater with ropes that stretch. Some ropes, for example of polyamide, become stiff and hard when overworked.

4.8 Before use, lifelines and gantlines, lizards and chairs should be load-tested to four or five times the loads they will be required to carry.

4.9 Some superficial splashing or wetting of lines by corrosive or rotting substances may be unavoidable during the progress of the work. The ropes etc chosen should not be susceptible to damage by the contaminant (see table p 88) and it should be sufficient to ensure that any effects of contamination are examined as soon as possible but in any case at the end of a day's work.

4.10 Mildew does not attack man-made fibre ropes but moulds can form on them. This will not affect their strength.

4.11 Eye or loop splices in ropes of polyamide or polyester materials should be made with four full tucks each with the completed strands of the rope followed by two tapered tucks for which the strands are halved and quartered for one tuck each respectively. Those portions of the splices containing the tucks with the reduced number of filaments should be securely wrapped with adhesive tape or other suitable material. Splices in polypropylene ropes should have at least three full tucks. The length of the splicing tails protruding from the finished splice should equal not less than three rope diameters.

4.12 Mechanical fastenings should not be used in lieu of splices on man-made fibre ropes because strands may be damaged during application of the mechanical fastening and the grip of the fastenings may be much affected by slight unavoidable fluctuations in the diameter of strands.

5 Portable ladders

5.1 A portable ladder should have a clear width of at least 255 mm (10 inches), be soundly constructed and have adequate strength for the purpose for which it is used. A ladder should not be used if any part is defective, for example if any rung depends for support solely on nails, spikes or similar improvisations.

5.2 All ladders should be inspected at regular intervals and maintained in sound condition. Wooden ladders should not be painted nor treated so as to hide cracks and defects.

5.3 When not in use, portable ladders should be stowed in a dry ventilated space away from heat.

5.4 A ladder in use should rise to a height of at least 1 metre (39 inches) above the top landing place unless there are other suitable handholds.

5.5 A portable ladder, whether rope or rigid type, must be adequately secured against displacement as near as possible to its upper resting place.

5.6 There should be a clearance of at least 150 mm behind all rungs.

5.7 Rigid portable ladders should be pitched at a safe angle between 65° and 70° to the horizontal (ie a slope of about one horizontal for four vertical). They should stand on a firm base and be lashed in position.

5.8 Planks should not be supported on the rungs of portable ladders to be used as a staging, nor should ladders be used horizontally for the same purpose.

5.9 A man negotiating a ladder needs both hands free; he should not attempt to carry tools or equipment in his hands. If he is wearing gloves or his hands are greasy, he must take extra care.

5.10 Working from ladders should be avoided as far as practicable since there is a risk of overbalancing and falling. Where it is necessary, a safety harness with a lifeline secured above the position of work should be worn when working at a height in excess of 2 metres (6½ feet) (see section 1.3).

CHAPTER 16

Anchoring, mooring and casting off

1 Anchoring

1.1 Before anchors are let go, a check should be made that there are no small craft or obstacles under the bow.

1.2 The man operating the brake and others in the vicinity should wear safety goggles and safety helmets to avoid the risk of injuries from dirt and rust particles and debris thrown off as the chain pays out.

1.3 Instructions given by portable transceivers (walkie-talkies) should always be identified with the ship, preferably by including her name in the instruction.

1.4 Seamen engaged in stowing an anchor cable into the locker should stand in a protected position and as far as practicable should keep in constant communication with the windlass operator.

1.5 Anchors housed and not required should be properly secured to guard against accidents or damage should the windlass brake be released inadvertently.

2 Characteristics of man-made fibre ropes

2.1 Safe handling of man-made fibre ropes requires techniques which differ from those for handling natural fibre ropes.

2.2 Man-made fibre ropes are relatively stronger than those of natural fibre and so for any given breaking strain have appreciably smaller circumferences, but wear or damage will diminish strength to a greater extent than would the same amount of wear or damage on a natural fibre rope. Recommendations for substitution of natural fibre ropes by man-made fibre ropes are given in the following table:

Manila		Polyamide (Nylon) etc		Polyester (Terylene etc)		Polypropylene	
Dia	Size	Dia	Size	Dia	Size	Dia	Size
48 mm	(6)	48 mm	(6)	48 mm	(6)	48 mm	(6)
56 mm	(7)	48 mm	(6)	48 mm	(6)	52 mm	(6½)
64 mm	(8)	52 mm	(6½)	52 mm	(6½)	56 mm	(7)
72 mm	(9)	60 mm	(7½)	60 mm	(7½)	64 mm	(8)
80 mm	(10)	64 mm	(8)	64 mm	(8)	72 mm	(9)
88 mm	(11)	72 mm	(9)	72 mm	(9)	80 mm	(10)
96 mm	(12)	80 mm	(10)	80 mm	(10)	88 mm	(11)
112 mm	(14)	88 mm	(11)	88 mm	(11)	96 mm	(12)

Diameter given for 3-strand, size no for 8-strand plaited.

Polyamide (nylon) or polyester ropes are recommended for mooring tails and should have a minimum finished length of 11 metres (6 fathoms) in order to provide the necessary elasticity. The strength of the tail when new should be approximately 25 per cent greater than that of the mooring rope or wire.

2.3 Man-made fibre ropes have high durability and low water absorption and are very resistant to rot or mildew but should not be left unduly long exposed to sunlight when not in use. They should be covered by tarpaulins or, if the ship is on a long voyage, stowed away.

2.4 Ropes should be kept free of contamination by chemicals (rust removers and paint strippers may be particularly damaging) and not stowed close to any source of heat. Any accidental contamination should be reported immediately for cleansing or other action to be taken (see also Chapter 15, section 4).

2.5 Careful inspection of man-made fibre ropes for wear externally and internally is necessary. A high degree of powdering observed between strands indicates excessive wear and reduced strength. Ropes with high stretch suffer greater interstrand wear than others. Hardness and stiffness in some ropes, polyamide (nylon) in particular, may also indicate overworking.

2.6 Man-made fibre stoppers of like material (but not polyamide) should be used on man-made fibre mooring lines, preferably using the 'West Country' method (double and reverse stoppering).

2.7 Unlike natural fibre ropes, man-made fibre ropes give little or no audible warning of approaching breaking-point.

2.8 Stretch imparted to man-made fibre ropes, which may be up to double that of natural fibre rope, is usually recovered almost instantaneously when tension is released. A break in the rope may therefore result in a dangerous back-lash and an item of running gear breaking loose may be projected with lethal force. Snatching of such ropes should be avoided; where it may occur inadvertently, personnel should stand well clear of the danger areas. The possibility of a mooring or towing rope parting under load is reduced by proper care, inspection and maintenance and by its proper use in service.

2.9 Man-made fibre ropes may easily be damaged by melting if frictional heat is generated during use. Too much friction on a warping drum may fuse the rope with consequential sticking and jumping of turns, which can be dangerous. Polypropylene is more liable to soften than other material. To avoid fusing, ropes should not be surged unnecessarily on winch barrels. For this reason, a minimum of turns should be used on the winch barrel; three turns are usually enough but on whelped drums one or two extra turns may be needed to ensure a good grip; these should be removed as soon as practicable.

2.10 The method of making eye splices in ropes of man-made fibres should be chosen according to the material of the rope:

(a) polyamide (nylon) and polyester fibre ropes need four full tucks in the splice each with the completed strands of the rope followed by two tapered tucks for which the strands are halved and quartered for one tuck each respectively. The length of the splicing tail protruding from the finished splice should be equal to at least three rope diameters. The portions of the splice containing the tucks with reduced number of filaments should be securely wrapped with adhesive-tape or other suitable material;

(b) polypropylene ropes should have at least three but not more than four full tucks in the splice. The protruding spliced tails should be equal to three rope diameters at least;

(c) polyethylene ropes should have four full tucks in the splice with protruding tails of three rope diameters at least.

3 Mooring

3.1 Surfaces of fairleads, bollards, bitts and drum ends should be kept clean and maintained in good condition. Rollers and fairleads should turn smoothly and a visual check made that corrosion has not weakened them.

3.2 Mooring decks should have anti-slip surfaces provided by fixed treads or by treatment with anti-slip paint.

3.3 A mooring rope should be examined frequently throughout its length for both external wear and wear between strands. Splices should be intact.

3.4 Wire ropes should be regularly treated with suitable lubricants.

3.5 New rope, 3-strand fibre rope and wire should be taken out of a coil in such fashion as to avoid disturbing the lay of the rope.

3.6 When wire is joined to a natural or man-made fibre rope, a thimble or other device should be inserted in the eye of the fibre rope; both wire and rope should have the same direction of lay.

3.7 A wire rope should not be used directly from a reel, unless designed for the purpose, because if the wire fouls the reel, both the reel and frame may be torn from the deck and cause injuries. Sufficient slack rope should be taken off a reel to cover all contingencies of use and be flaked out on deck in a safe manner. If there is doubt of the amount required, then the complete wire should be removed from the reel. Paying out of the wire rope should be controlled by turns round bitts or drum ends.

3.8 When cargo winches are used for handling springs on the main deck, suitable leads should be provided. If it is necessary to use a snatch block, precautions should be taken against its breaking loose.

3.9 A watchman, rigger or boatman should normally be employed to heave mooring ropes ashore. No seaman should go ashore other than by safe means.

3.10 A sufficient number of men must always be available at each end of the ship during mooring operations.

3.11 A seaman should not in any circumstances stand in a bight of rope nor, whenever avoidable, in the bight formed between the drum and the fairlead.

3.12 An experienced seaman should be at the winch controls throughout the whole time of the mooring operation.

3.13 When ropes and wires are under strain, as in towing, all persons should remain in positions of safety to the fullest possible extent.

3.14 Immediate action should be taken to reduce the load should any part of the system appear to be under excessive strain.

3.15 The safe method of heaving by means of turns on a drum is for one man to be stationed at the drum end with a second man backing and coiling down the slack as it is taken in.

3.16 Sharp-angled leads of rope or wire should always be avoided.

3.17 A wire should never be led across a fibre rope on a bollard. Wires and ropes should be kept in separate fairleads or bollards.

3.18 Wire on the drum end of a winch should not be used as a check wire.

3.19 When a wire is used as a slip wire, the eyes should be seized.

3.20 Chain stoppers should be used for stoppering off wire mooring ropes. They should be applied with two half-hitches in the form of a cow hitch suitably spaced with the tail backed against the lay of the wire to ensure that the chain neither jams nor opens up the lay of the wire.

4 Mooring to buoys

4.1 Where mooring to buoys is undertaken from a ship's launch or boat, seamen engaged in the operation should wear lifejackets and a lifebuoy with attached lifeline should be kept readily available in the boat.

4.2 Means should be provided to enable a man who has fallen into the water to climb back on board the launch or boat. If a boarding ladder with flexible sides is used, it should be weighted so that the lower rungs remain below the surface.

4.3 Where mooring to buoys is undertaken directly from the ship, a lifebuoy with attached line of sufficient length should be available for immediate use.

4.4 When slip wires are used for mooring to buoys or dolphins, the eyes of the wires should never be put over the bitts.

5 Casting off

5.1 A sufficient number of men should always be available at each end of the ship during casting off.

5.2 When no mooring gangs are available, a slip wire or mooring rope on the bight should be utilised for letting go.

5.3 Tow lines should be let go in a controlled fashion and seamen should keep well clear of the eyes of tow ropes.

CHAPTER 17

Lifting and mechanical handling appliances

1 General

1.1 All appliances and gear used for lifting, lowering and handling loads on a ship should be inspected, examined and, where necessary, tested at regular intervals. Particulars of inspections, examinations and tests carried out should always be kept up to date. Inspections, examinations and tests should be carried out by a competent person.

1.2 Appliances and gear should be marked where appropriate with their safe working loads.

1.3 Any lifting or handling appliance or gear that has not been subject to regular inspection, examination or test, or is in any way defective, should not be used at any time. Any defects arising in the course of use should be reported promptly and operations suspended.

1.4 Inexperienced seamen and those less than 18 years of age should not be in sole charge of any powered lifting or handling appliance. If under instruction, they should be closely supervised by a competent person for the whole time.

1.5 Controls of lifting and handling appliances should be permanently and legibly marked with their function and their operating directions shown by arrows or other simple means, indicating the position for hoisting or lowering, slewing or luffing etc.

1.6 Make-shift extensions should not be fitted to controls nor any unauthorised alterations made to them. Foot-operated controls should have slip-resistant surfaces.

1.7 No lifting appliance should be used with any locking pawl, safety attachment or device rendered inoperative. If, exceptionally, limit switches need to be isolated in order to lower a crane to its stowage position, the utmost care should be taken to ensure the operation is completed safely.

1.8 A powered appliance should always have a man at the controls while it is in operation; it should never be left to run with a control secured in the ON position.

1.9 If any powered appliance is to be left unattended with the power on, loads should be taken off and controls put in 'neutral' or 'off' positions. Where practical, controls should be locked or otherwise inactivated to prevent accidental restarting. When work is completed, power should be shut off.

1.10 The person operating any lifting or handling appliance should have no other duties which might interfere with his primary task. He should be in a proper and protected position, facing controls and, so far as is practicable, with a clear view of the whole operation.

1.11 If the operator of a lifting or handling device does not have a full unobstructed view of the operation, a signaller should be posted having no other duties. He should be an experienced seaman and not less than 18 years of age. No other person should give signals.

1.12 The signals shown on page 100 should be used when working winches, cranes or derricks.

1.13 Before any attempt is made to free equipment that has become jammed under load, every effort should first be made to take off the load safely. Precautions should be taken to guard against sudden or unexpected freeing. Others not directly engaged in the operation should keep in safe or protected positions.

2 Winches and cranes

2.1 The drum end of wire runners or falls should be secured to winch barrels or crane drums by proper clamps or U-bolts. The

Code of hand signals when working winches, cranes or derricks.

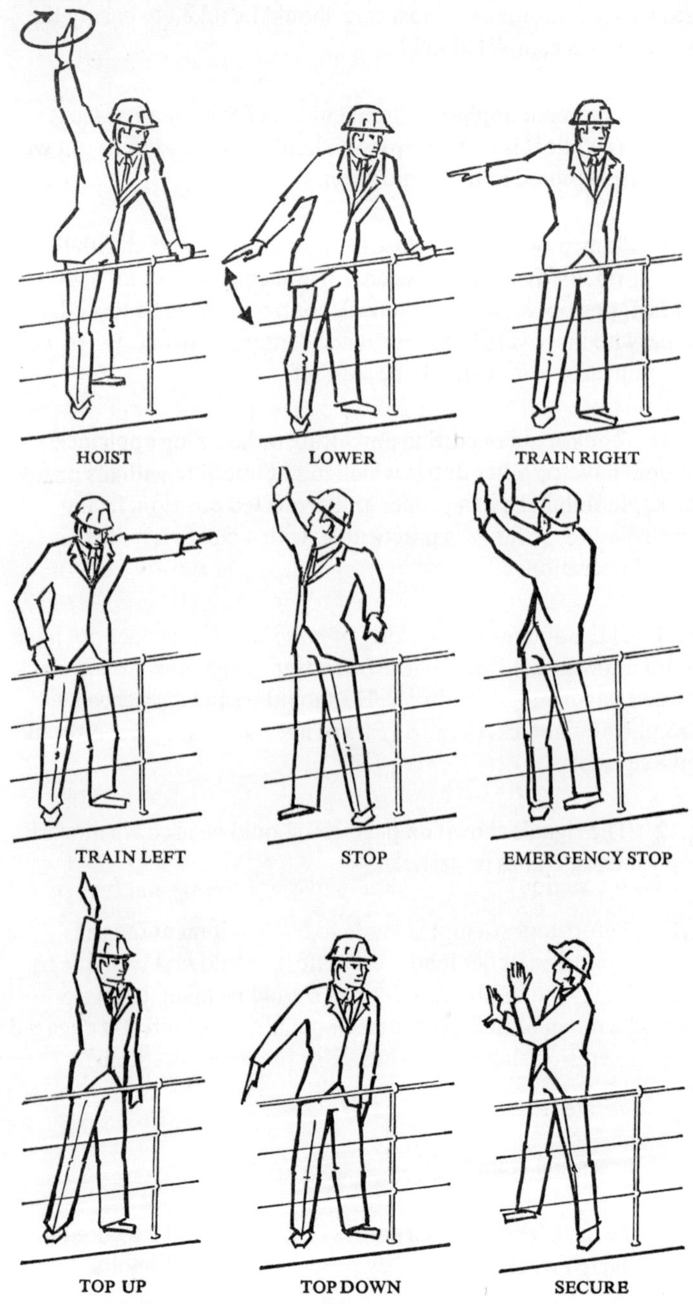

HOIST | LOWER | TRAIN RIGHT

TRAIN LEFT | STOP | EMERGENCY STOP

TOP UP | TOP DOWN | SECURE

runner or fall should be long enough to leave at least 3 turns on the barrel or drum at maximum normal extension.

2.2 Slack turns of wire or rope on a barrel or drum should be avoided as they are likely to pull out suddenly under load.

2.3 When a winch is changed from single to double gear or vice versa, any load should be first released and the clutch should be secured so that it cannot become disengaged when the winch is working.

2.4 Steam winches should be so maintained that the operator is not exposed to the risk of scalding by leaks of hot water and steam.

2.5 Before a steam winch is operated, the cylinders and steam pipes should be cleared of water by opening the appropriate drain cocks. The stop valve between winch and deck steam line should be kept unobstructed.

2.6 When a travelling crane is moved, any necessary holding bolts or clamps should be replaced before the crane is operated in its new position.

2.7 Access to a crane should be always by the proper means provided.

3 Derricks

3.1 This section applies generally to the conventional type of ship's derrick. For other types, such as the 'Hallen' and 'Stulken' derricks, the manufacturer's instructions should be followed.

3.2 Runner guides should be fitted to all derricks so that when the runner is slack, the bight is not a hazard to persons walking along the decks. Where rollers are fitted to runner guides, they should rotate freely.

3.3 Before a derrick is raised or lowered, all persons on deck in the vicinity should be warned so that no person stands in, or is in danger from, bights of wire and other ropes. All necessary wires should be flaked out.

3.4 When a single span derrick is being raised, lowered or adjusted, the hauling part of the topping lift or bull-wire (ie winch end whip) should be adequately secured to the drum end.

3.5 The winch driver should raise or lower the derrick at a speed consistent with the safe handling of the guys.

3.6 Before a derrick is raised, lowered or adjusted with a topping lift purchase, the hauling part of the span should be flaked out for its entire length in a safe manner. A seaman should back up to assist the man controlling the wire on the drum and by keeping the wire clear of turns and in making fast to the bitts or cleats. Where the hauling part of a topping lift purchase is led to a derrick span winch, the bull-wire should be handled in the same way.

3.7 To secure the derrick in its final position, the topping lift purchase should be secured to bitts or cleats by first putting on three complete turns followed by four crossing turns and finally securing the whole with a lashing to prevent the turns jumping off due to the wire's natural springiness.

3.8 When a derrick is lowered on a topping lift purchase, a seaman should be detailed for lifting and holding the pawl bar, ready to release it should the need arise; the pawl should be fully engaged before the topping lift purchase or bull-wire is released. While employed on this duty the seaman should not attempt or be given any other task; in no circumstances should the pawl bar be wedged or lashed up.

3.9 A derrick having a topping winch, and particularly one that is self-powered, should not be topped hard against the mast, table or clamp in such a way that the initial heave required to free the pawl bar prior to lowering the derrick cannot be achieved in complete safety, that is, without putting an undue strain on the topping lift purchase and its attachments.

3.10 A heel block should be secured additionally by means of a chain or wire so that the block will be pulled into position under load but does not drop when the load is released.

3.11 The derrick should be lowered to the deck or crutch and properly secured whenever repairs or changes to the rig are to be carried out.

3.12 Cranes or derricks should not be used to drag heavy loads from under deck; where necessary winches should be used for such work. This does not apply to the normal working of general cargo when the angle is small and when there is an ample margin between the loads handled and the safe working load of the crane or derrick.

3.13 If heavy cargo is to be dragged under deck with ship's winches, the runner should be led directly from the heel block to avoid overloading the derrick boom and rigging. Where a heavy load is to be moved, a snatch block or bull wire should be used to provide a fair-lead for the runner and to keep the load clear of obstructions.

4 Union purchase

4.1 Where derricks have not been marked with the safe working load in union purchase they should not be used for loads in excess of one-third of the SWL of the derrick (or of the lower rated derrick where there are unequal ratings). It must be remembered that in general it is the SWL of the single runner and NOT that of the derrick which will determine the SWL of the union purchase.

4.2 The following precautions should be strictly taken to avoid excessive tensions:

(a) the angle between the married runners should not normally exceed 90° and an angle of 120° should never be exceeded;

(b) the cargo sling should be kept as short as possible so as to clear the bulwarks without the angle between the runners exceeding 90° (or 120° in special circumstances);

(c) derricks should be topped as high as practicable consistent with safe working;

(d) the derricks should not be rigged further apart than is absolutely necessary.

4.3 The following examples will show how rapidly excessive loads may be put on derricks, runners and attachments as the angle between runners increases:
At 60° included angle, the tension in each runner would be just over half the load; at 90° the tension would be nearly three-quarters of the load; at 120° the tension would be equal to the load; and at 175° the tension would be nearly 12 times the load.

4.4 When using union purchase, winch operators should wind in and pay out in step, otherwise dangerous tensions may develop in the rig.

4.5 An adequate preventer guy should always be rigged on the outboard side of each derrick when used in union purchase. The preventer guy should be looped over the head of the derrick, and as close to and parallel with the outboard guy as available fittings permit. Each guy should be secured to individual and adequate deck or other fastenings.

4.6 Narrow angles between derricks and outboard guys and between outboard guys and the vertical should be avoided in union purchase as these materially increase the loading on the guys. The angle between the outboard derrick and its outboard guy and preventer should not be too large as this may cause the outboard derrick to jack-knife. In general, the inboard derrick guys and preventer should be secured as nearly as possible at an angle of 90° to the derrick.

5 Stoppers

5.1 Where fitted, mechanical topping lift stoppers should be used. Where chain stoppers are used, they should ALWAYS be applied by two half-hitches in the form of a cow hitch suitably spaced with the remaining chain and rope tail backed round the wire and held taut to the wire.

5.2 A chain stopper should be shackled as near as possible in line with the span downhaul and always to an eyeplate, not passed round on a bight which would induce bending stresses similar to those in a knotted chain.

5.3 No stopper should be shackled to the same eyeplate as the lead block for the span downhaul; this is particularly hazardous when the lead block has to be turned to take the downhaul to the winch or secure it to bitts or cleats.

5.4 The span downhaul should always be eased to a stopper and the stopper should take the weight before turns are removed from the winch, bitts, or cleats.

6 Overhaul of cargo gear

6.1 When a cargo block or shackle is replaced, care should be taken to ensure that the replacement is of the correct type, size and safe working load necessary for its intended use.

6.2 All shackles should have their pins effectively secured or seized with wire.

6.3 A special check should be made on completion of the work to ensure that all the split pins in blocks etc have been replaced and secured.

6.4 On completion of the gear overhaul, all working places should be cleaned of oil or grease.

7 Mechanical handling appliances

7.1 Mechanical handling appliances such as fork lift trucks, etc, carried on board to assist in the handling of cargo should be periodically inspected, examined and tested as specified in section 1.1, and properly maintained. Appliances used for explosives should be approved for the purpose.

7.2 Trucks for lifting and transporting should be used only by competent persons and only when the ship is in still water; they should never be used when vessels are in a seaway since the vehicles cannot be adequately controlled when the vessel is pitching and rolling.

7.3 Appliances powered by internal combustion engines should not be used in enclosed spaces unless the spaces are adequately ventilated. The engine should not be left running when the truck is idle.

7.4 When not in use or left unattended whilst the vessel is in port, trucks for lifting and transporting should be aligned along the length of the ship with brakes on, operating controls locked, and, where applicable, the forks tilted forward flush with the deck and clear of the passageway. If the trucks are on an incline, their wheels should be chocked. If not to be used for some time, and at all times whilst at sea, appliances should be properly secured to prevent movement.

7.5 Before a truck is used, it should be checked to ensure that it is in a safe condition, that horns, brakes and controls are in good working order and, in particular, that pneumatic tyres where fitted are inflated to the correct pressure.

7.6 A truck should not be used to handle a load greater than its marked capacity or to move insecure or unsafe loads. Damaged or defective pallets or stillages should not be used. No attempt should be made to handle a heavy load by the simultaneous use of two trucks.

7.7 When the forward vision of the operator is obscured by the load, the appliance should be driven in reverse. Where this is impracticable, a signaller should be placed to control the movement.

7.8 Persons other than the driver should not be carried on a truck. Riding on the forks of a truck is particularly dangerous.

7.9 The driver should be careful to keep all parts of his body within the limits of the width of the truck or load.

CHAPTER 18

Hatches

1 General

1.1 Weather deck hatch covers and their securing arrangements should be inspected at regular intervals while the ship is at sea.

1.2 Beams and hatch covers should be properly maintained.

1.3 Broken, split, poorly-fitting or otherwise defective wooden hatch covers should be repaired or replaced as soon as possible.

1.4 Hatch covers should not be used for any other purpose.

1.5 When hatches are opened, the area around the openings should be adequately illuminated. Such illumination should be maintained for as long as the hatches remain open where there may be a risk of a person falling into the space.

1.6 Unless hatches are fitted with coamings to a height of at least 760 mm (30 inches) they should be securely covered or fenced to a height of 1 metre (39 inches) when not in use for the passage of cargo.

1.7 Work should not be done nor loads imposed over any section of wooden hatchboards unless all supporting beams are in place, and a competent person should satisfy himself that the hatch cover can safely support any load to be placed on it.

2 Handling and stowage of non-mechanical hatch covers and beams

2.1 When hauling tarpaulins seamen should walk forwards and NOT backwards so that they can see where they are walking.

2.2 Hatch covers and beams should not be removed or replaced while work is going on below them.

2.3 Hatch covers should not be handled manually unless they can be easily lifted by two men. One man should not attempt to handle hatchboards unaided.

2.4 Four-legged slings should be used for lifting pontoons, slab hatches etc.

2.5 Beam slings should be of adequate length to reach the lifting points of the beams without forming enclosed angles in excess of 120°. They should be secure against accidental dislodgement.

2.6 Each leg of all beam and pontoon slings should be fitted with a suitable rope lanyard at least 3 metres (10 feet) long to control swinging.

2.7 When removing hatchboards, seamen should work from the centre towards the sides and, when replacing them, from the sides towards the centre.

2.8 Beams remaining in position in a partly opened hatchway should be secured against accidental displacement. If that cannot be done, they should be removed.

2.9 Immediately before beams are to be removed, a check should be made that pins or other locking devices have been freed.

2.10 The head of a crane or derrick being used to lift beams should be directly over them to avoid swing when beams clear their sockets.

2.11 When beams, pontoons and slab hatches are being lifted mechanically, one man alone should be responsible for directing the winch operator.

2.12 Beams that have become jammed at an angle should be freed with care.

2.13 No one should walk out on a beam for any purpose whatsoever.

2.14 Hatch covers, beams, pontoons and tarpaulins which have been removed should be properly stacked and secured or placed in such a manner that they cannot fall or otherwise cause danger. Where practicable a space of at least 1 metre (39 inches) should be left between them and the hatchway.

2.15 Where practicable, hatch covers should be arranged in neat piles away from the hatchway or laid singly on deck with no gaps between them. They should be properly handled and not thrown.

2.16 Beams and hatch boards, unless made to be interchangeable, should be replaced in proper order according to hatch, deck and section marked on them.

2.17 Each beam and hatch board should be properly seated.

2.18 A marline spike, or something similar, should be used to test the alignment of the pinholes for securing beams. Fingers should not be used for this purpose.

2.19 When covering a hatch, a check should be made to ensure that the hatch boards completely cover the hatch or hatch section for which they are intended so that no dangerous gaps are left.

2.20 Before covers of a hatch are replaced a check should be made that all persons are out of the hold or clear of the hatchway.

3 Mechanical hatch covers

3.1 Instructions for the safe operation of mechanical hatch covers should be posted up in a prominent position. In all cases, these instructions should be followed and those engaged in the work should be aware of any potential dangers accompanying the operation. Only the jacks or other means provided by the manufacturers should be used for raising or lowering the covers.

3.2 All types of mechanical hatch cover should be opened and closed with due care and attention under the direct supervision of a ship's officer or experienced petty officer. All persons should keep clear of the hatch and stowage position during the operation of the covers. The area should be clear of guys, dunnage, runners etc which might foul the covers.

3.3 No one should climb on to closed or stowed hatch covers without checking that they are properly secured. No person should remain on or near the covers when they are being moved or when they are partially open.

3.4 Mechanical hatch covers in the open position should be secured against movement using chain preventers or other suitable means.

CHAPTER 19

Work in cargo spaces

1 Access

1.1 Cargo spaces should always be well ventilated before entry is made. Should it be necessary to enter a hold with a suspect atmosphere, the operation should be continuously supervised and the procedures set out in Chapter 10 'Entry into enclosed spaces' followed.

1.2 Whenever practicable, the permanent means of access should be used. In other cases, portable rigid ladders should be used (see Chapter 15, section 5). When necessary, lifelines and safety harness should be available and used.

1.3 Should it be necessary to remove injured persons from a hold, the best available method should be adopted but where practicable all access openings should be opened and the following equipment used where available:

(a) a manually-operated davit, suitably secured over the access opening;

(b) a cage or stretcher fitted with controlling lines at the lower end.

1.4 When hatches are opened, there should be ample clearance for any loads which may have to be raised or lowered.

2 Lighting in cargo spaces

2.1 Cargo spaces in which work has to be undertaken should be adequately lit. Dazzle and strong contrasts of light and shadow should be avoided.

2.2 Open or naked lights should not be used. Portable lights, when used, should be adequately guarded and suitable for the intended purpose.

2.3 Portable lights should not be lowered nor suspended by their cables. Leads for portable lights should be kept clear of loads, running gear and moving equipment.

2.4 Portable lights should be properly secured against accidental displacement.

2.5 Lights should not be switched off nor removed before it has been ascertained that all seamen are clear of the compartment or hold.

3 Fencing

3.1 Before work is done in cargo spaces, all openings through which a person may fall should be adequately guarded or fenced (see Chapter 9, section 5).

3.2 Guard rails should be tight with stanchions secured in position, and properly maintained.

3.3 Partly opened unguarded hatches should never be covered with tarpaulins; this would present a very dangerous situation which would not be apparent to a person walking across the hatch.

4 General precautions

4.1 Care should be taken when walking over dunnage which is loosely stowed or from which nails may be protruding.

4.2 When work is to be done near a tall stack of cargo, the cargo should be secured to prevent it falling. If the stack is of bagged cargo, damage to the bags may cause bleeding and subsequent collapse of the stow.

4.3 Where it is necessary to mount the face of a stow, a portable ladder should be used.

4.4 When work is being done on a tall stack of cargo or in places where there is a risk of falling, a safety net should be erected. It should not be secured to hatch covers.

CHAPTER 20

Work in machinery spaces

1 General

1.1 Every dangerous part of any machinery should be securely fenced unless it is in such a position or of such construction as to be safe to all crew.

1.2 All steam pipes, exhaust pipes and fittings which by their location and temperature present a hazard, should be adequately lagged or otherwise shielded. The insulation of heated surfaces should be properly maintained, particularly in the vicinity of oil systems.

1.3 Personnel required to work in machinery spaces which have high noise levels should wear suitable hearing protectors (see Chapter 5, section 3).

1.4 Where high noise level in a machinery space or the wearing of hearing protectors may mask an audible alarm, a visual alarm of suitable intensity should be provided, where practicable, to attract attention and indicate that an audible alarm is sounding. This should preferably take the form of a light or lights with rotating reflectors.

1.5 The source of any oil leakage should be located and repaired as soon as practicable.

1.6 Waste oil should not be allowed to accumulate in the bilges or on tank tops. Any accumulation should be disposed of in accordance with Oil Pollution Regulations at the earliest opportunity. Tank tops and bilges should, wherever practicable, be painted a light colour and kept clean and well-illuminated in the vicinity of pressure oil pipes so that leaks may be readily located.

1.7 Great caution is required when filling any settling or other oil tank to prevent it overflowing, especially in an engine room where exhaust pipes or other hot surfaces are directly below.

1.8 Particular care should be taken when filling tanks which have their sounding pipes in the machinery spaces to ensure that weighted cocks are closed. In no case should a weighted cock on a fuel or lubricating oil tank sounding pipe or on a fuel or lubricating oil tank gauge be secured in the open position.

1.9 Engine room bilges should at all times be kept clear of rubbish and other substances so that mud-boxes are not blocked and the bilges may be readily and easily pumped.

1.10 Remote controls fitted for stopping machinery or pumps or for operating oil-settling tank quick-closing valves in the event of fire, should be tested regularly to ensure that they are functioning satisfactorily.

2 Boilers

2.1 A notice should be displayed at each boiler setting out operating instructions. Information provided by the manufacturers of the oil-burning equipment should be displayed in the boiler room.

2.2 To avoid the danger of a blowback when lighting boilers, the correct flashing up procedure should always be followed:

(a) there should be no loose oil on the furnace floor;

(b) the oil should be at the correct temperature for the grade of oil being used; if not, the temperature of the oil must be regulated before lighting is attempted;

(c) the furnace should be blown through with air to clear any oil vapour;

(d) the torch, specially provided for the purpose, should always be used for lighting a burner unless an adjacent burner in the same furnace is already lit; other means of ignition, such as introducing loose burning material into the furnace, should not be used. An explosion may result from attempts to relight a burner from the hot brickwork of the furnace;

(e) if all is in order, the operator should stand to one side, and the lighted torch inserted and fuel turned on. Care should be taken that there is not too much oil on the torch which could drip and possibly cause a fire;

(f) if the oil does not light immediately, the fuel supply should be turned off and the furnace ventilated by allowing air to blow through for two or three minutes to clear any oil vapour before a second attempt to light is made. During this interval the burner should be removed and the atomiser and tip inspected to verify that they are in good order;

(g) if, while the burner is alight, there is a total flame failure in the furnace, the fuel supply should be turned off.

2.3 The avenues of escape from the boiler fronts and firing spaces should be kept clear.

2.4 Where required to be fitted, the gauge glass cover should always be in place when the glass is under pressure. If a gauge glass or cover needs to be replaced or repaired, the gauge should be shut off and drained before the cover is removed.

3 Unmanned machinery spaces

3.1 A seafarer should never enter or remain in an unmanned machinery space alone, unless he has received permission from, or been instructed by the engineer officer in charge at the time. Before entering the space, at regular intervals whilst in the space, and on having finally left the space, he must report by telephone, or other means provided, to the duty deck officer. The foregoing also applies to the engineer officer in charge. A seafarer may only be instructed to enter an unmanned machinery space alone by the designated engineer officer in charge and then he may only be sent to carry out a specific task which he may be expected to complete in a comparatively short time. Before he enters the space the method of reporting should be clearly explained and should follow the lines indicated above. On leaving the space he must also report in person to the designated engineer officer in charge. Consideration should be given in appropriate instances to using a 'permit-to-work' (see Chapter 7).

3.2 Notices of safety precautions to be observed by persons working in unmanned machinery spaces should be clearly displayed at all entrances to the space. Warning should be given that in unmanned machinery spaces there is a likelihood of machinery suddenly starting up.

3.3 Unmanned machinery spaces should be adequately illuminated at all times.

3.4 When machinery is under bridge control, the bridge should always be advised when a change in machinery setting is contemplated by the engine room staff, and before a reversion to engine room control of the machinery.

4 Refrigeration machinery

4.1 Adequate information should be available on each vessel, laying down the operating and maintenance safeguards of the refrigeration plant, the particular properties of the refrigerant and the precautions for its safe handling.

4.2 No one should enter a refrigerated compartment without first informing a responsible officer.

4.3 The compartment or flat in which refrigeration machinery is fitted should be adequately ventilated and illuminated. Where ventilation cannot be carried out efficiently by natural means, mechanical ventilation should be employed as necessary, arranged so that the machines are situated between inlets and outlets and that the air is exhausted from both the top and bottom of the compartment. Refrigerating machinery spaces within crew accommodation to which the *Merchant Shipping (Crew Accommodation) Regulations 1978* apply are required to be ventilated by at least two ventilators to the open air, one of which must be fitted with an exhaust fan and have its inlet near the bottom of the space.

4.4 Where fitted, both the supply and exhaust fans to and from compartments in which refrigeration machinery is situated should be kept running at all times. Inlets and outlets should be kept unobstructed. When there is any doubt as to the adequacy of the ventilation, a portable fan or other suitable means should be used to assist in the removal of toxic gases from the immediate vicinity of the machine.

4.5 Should it be known or suspected that the refrigerant has leaked into any compartments, no attempt should be made to enter those compartments until a responsible officer has been advised of the situation. If it is necessary to enter the space, it should be ventilated to the fullest extent practicable and the person entering should wear approved breathing apparatus. A man should be stationed in constant attendance outside the space, also with breathing apparatus (see Chapter 10).

CHAPTER 21

Hydraulic and pneumatic equipment

1 General

1.1 Personnel using hydraulic and pneumatic equipment should be fully conversant with the proper procedures for its safe operation. Operating instructions should be followed at all times.

1.2 Operators should ensure that the system operating pressure shown on the pressure gauge is at the level recommended.

1.3 The equipment should not be operated if it is in any way faulty or when a safety device is missing, incorrectly adjusted or defective.

1.4 The equipment, if defective in any respect, should be effectively immobilised pending adjustment or repair. Only authorised personnel should undertake repairs to the equipment or adjustment of the pressure settings of safety devices (see Chapter 22, section 12).

1.5 Prior to a hydraulic system being activated and when it is being closed down, the recommended checks should be made to ensure that there are no pockets of air or trapped pressure in the system and that there are no external leaks. Air pockets trapped in the system cause erratic action which can lead to injury or to damage to the installations or equipment.

1.6 Only the correct grade of hydraulic fluid should be used for topping up a hydraulic system.

1.7 Any spillage of hydraulic fluid should be cleared up immediately. Some fluids are based on mineral oils and any such fluid on the skin should be thoroughly washed off (see Chapter 1, section 2.8).

1.8 Where flexible hose assemblies are used, the application of a line of light coloured paint overlapping the junction of ferrule and hose will enable movement between the two to be readily noticed in advance of a failure.

1.9 When the equipment is in use, operators should never reach through a linkage of any hydraulically operated mechanism to set, adjust or operate the controls.

1.10 Before pressure is released from a system, any load on it should, where necessary, be adequately supported by other means. The operator should ensure that all pressures have been released before disconnecting any line, plug, valve or other component.

2 Hydraulic jacks

2.1 Jacks should be inspected before use to ensure that they are in a sound condition and that the oil in the reservoir reaches the minimum recommended level.

2.2 Before a jack is operated, care should be taken to ensure that it has an adequate lifting capability for the work for which it is to be used and that its foundation is level and of adequate strength.

2.3 Jacks should be applied only to the recommended or safe jacking points on equipment.

2.4 Equipment under which personnel are required to work should be properly supported with chocks, wedges or by other safe means – never by jacks alone.

2.5 Jack operating handles should be removed if possible when not required to be in position for raising or lowering the jack.

CHAPTER 22

Overhaul of machinery

1 General

1.1 Before any repair or maintenance work is commenced, care should be taken to ensure that all measures and precautions necessary for the safety of those concerned have been taken (see Chapter 7 on 'permit-to-work' systems).

1.2 No maintenance work or repair which might affect the supply of water to the fire main or sprinkler system should be started without the prior permission of the Master and Chief Engineer.

1.3 No alarm system should be isolated without the permission of the Chief Engineer.

1.4 Before machinery is serviced or repaired, measures should be taken to prevent turning or inadvertent starting as may occur with automatic or remote control systems.

1.5 Electrically-operated machinery should be isolated from the power supply.

1.6 Steam-operated machinery should have both steam and exhaust valves securely closed and, where possible, locked off.

1.7 In all cases, warning notices should be posted at or near the controls giving warning that the machinery concerned is not to be used.

1.8 When valves or filter covers have to be removed or similar operations have to be performed on pressurised systems, that part of the system should be isolated by closing the appropriate valves. Drain cocks should be opened to ensure that pressure is off the system.

1.9 When joints of pipes, fittings etc are being broken, the fastenings should not be completely removed until the joint has been broken and it has been established that no pressure remains within.

1.10 Before a section of the steam pipe system is opened to the steam supply, all drains should be opened. Steam should be admitted very slowly and the drains kept open until all the water has been expelled.

1.11 The officer in charge should give careful consideration to the hazards involved before allowing maintenance or repairs to, or immediately adjacent to, moving machinery. This should be permitted only in circumstances where no danger exists or where it is impracticable for the machinery to be stopped. The person who is to carry out the work should wear close-fitting clothing. Long hair should be covered (see Chapter 5, section 2.5). The officer in charge should consider whether it is necessary in the interests of safety for a second person to be in close attendance whilst the work is being carried out.

1.12 Heavy parts of dismantled machinery temporarily put aside should be firmly secured against movement in a seaway and, as far as practicable, be clear of walkways. Sharp projections on them should be covered when reasonably practicable.

1.13 Means of access to fire fighting equipment, emergency escape routes and watertight doors should never be obstructed.

1.14 Spare gear, tools and other equipment or material should never be left lying around, especially near to stabiliser or steering gear rams and switchboards.

1.15 A marline spike, steel rod, or other suitable device should be used to align holes in machinery being reassembled or mounted; fingers should never be used.

1.16 When guards or other safety devices have been removed from machinery to facilitate the overhaul, they should be replaced immediately the work is completed and before the machinery or equipment is tested.

1.17 An approved safety lamp should always be used for illuminating spaces where oil or oil vapour is present. Vapour should be dispersed by ventilation before work is done.

2 Protective clothing and equipment

2.1 Safety helmets should be worn by those engaged in the overhaul of engineroom machinery where there is a risk of head injury and by others necessarily working in the area who might be struck by falling objects.

2.2 Seafarers required to work in machinery spaces which have high noise levels should wear suitable hearing protection.

2.3 Suitable eye protection should always be worn by those handling chemicals or welding, grinding, scaling, hammering, using a cold chisel or doing any other work of a similar nature.

2.4 If essential maintenance or repair work necessitates the removal of asbestos lagging, the precautions set out in Chapter 1, section 2.19 should be adopted.

2.5 Spilled oil should always be cleared up immediately as a matter of habit, but floor plates will still become slippery making footholds insecure. This should be kept in mind during any work in machinery spaces where a lurch or fall could cause injury and particularly when heavy items of machinery are being handled. Risks are reduced by the wearing of suitable safety footwear with slip-resistant soles.

2.6 Protective clothing and equipment are described in Chapter 5.

3 Lifting

3.1 Where practicable, all items of lifting gear should be marked with safe working loads and not intentionally subjected to loads in excess of the rating. Lifting appliances which are not marked with their safe working load, should not be used (see Chapter 17, section 1).

3.2 When machinery and, in particular, pistons are to be lifted by means of screw-in eye-bolts, the eye-bolts should be checked to ensure that they have collars, that the threads are in good condition and that the bolts are screwed hard down on to their collars. Screw holes for lifting bolts in piston heads should be cleaned and the threads checked to see that they are not wasted before the bolts are inserted.

4 Floor plates and hand rails

4.1 Where provided, lifting handles should be used when a floor plate is removed or replaced. When lifting handles are not available, the plate should be levered up with a suitable tool and a chock inserted before lifting. On no account should fingers be used to prise up the edges.

4.2 Whenever floor plates or handrails are removed, warning notices should be posted, the openings should be effectively fenced or guarded and the area well-illuminated.

5 Working aloft or over bottom platforms

5.1 A stage or ladder should always be used when working beyond normal reach (see Chapter 15,).

5.2 When work is done at a level above the bottom platform, precautions should be taken against heavy objects such as tools or parts of machinery falling on a person below. A firmly secured bucket or box should be used to hold tools and loose parts of machinery.

6 Boilers

6.1 Boilers should be opened only under the direction of an engineer officer. Care should be taken to check, after emptying, that the vacuum is broken before manhole doors are removed. Even if an air cock has been opened to break the vacuum, the practice should always be to loosen the manhole door nuts and break the joint before the removal of the dogs and knocking in the doors. The top manhole doors should be removed first.

Personnel should stand clear of hot vapour when doors are opened.

6.2 No person should enter any boiler, boiler furnace or boiler flue until it has cooled sufficiently to make work in such places safe.

6.3 Before entry is permitted to a boiler which is part of a range of two or more boilers, the engineer officer in charge should ensure that either:

(a) all inlets through which steam or water might enter the boiler from any other part of the range have been disconnected, drained and left open to atmosphere; or, where that is not practicable;

(b) all valves or cocks, including blowdown valves controlling entry of steam or water, have been closed and securely locked, and notices posted to prevent them being opened again until authorisation is given.

The above precautions should be maintained whilst personnel remain in the boiler.

6.4 Every boiler, boiler furnace or boiler flue, should be adequately ventilated before anyone enters and while persons remain inside. An attendant should always be standing by outside while persons remain inside the boiler.

6.5 Men cleaning tubes, scaling boilers, and cleaning backends, should wear appropriate protective clothing and equipment including goggles and respirators.

6.6 Special care should be exercised before a boiler is entered which has not been in use for some time or where chemicals have been used to prevent rust forming. The atmosphere may be deficient in oxygen and tests should be carried out before any person is allowed to enter. See Chapter 10 for advice on entering enclosed spaces.

7 Auxiliary machinery and equipment

7.1 Before work is started on an electric generator or auxiliary machine, the machine should be stopped and the starting air valve or similar device should be secured so that it cannot be operated.

A notice should be posted warning that the machine is not to be started nor the turning gear used. To avoid the danger of motoring and electric shock to any person working on the machine, it should be isolated electrically from the switchboard or starter before work is commenced. The circuit-breaker should be opened and a notice posted at the switchboard warning personnel that the breaker is not to be closed. Where practicable, the circuit-breaker should be locked open.

7.2 No attempt should be made to start a diesel engine without first barring round with the indicator cocks open. The barring gear should then be disengaged before starting the engine.

7.3 Oily deposits or flammable material should never be allowed to be present in way of diesel engine relief valves, crankcase explosion doors or scavenge belt safety discs.

7.4 Flammable coatings should never be applied to the internal surfaces of air starting reservoirs.

7.5 Care should be taken to prevent the jets from a diesel engine fuel injector impinging on the skin during testing. Leakage from other high pressure parts of injection equipment is similarly dangerous.

7.6 Oxygen should on no account be used for starting engines. To do so would probably cause a violent explosion.

8 Main engines

8.1 Where necessary, suitable staging, adequately secured, should be used to provide a working platform.

8.2 Before anyone is allowed to enter or work in the main engine crankcase or gear case, the turning gear should be engaged and a warning notice posted at the starting position.

8.3 Before the main engine turning gear is used, a check should be made to ensure that all personnel are clear of the crankcase and of any moving part of the main engine and that the duty deck officer has confirmed that the propeller is clear.

8.4 If a hot bearing has been detected in a closed crankcase, the crankcase should not be opened until sufficient time has been allowed for the bearing to cool down, otherwise the entry of air could create an explosive air/oil vapour mixture.

8.5 The opened crankcase or gear case should be well-ventilated to expel all flammable gases before any source of ignition, such as a portable lamp (unless of an approved safety type) is brought near to it.

8.6 Before the main engine is restarted, a responsible engineer officer should check that the shaft is clear and inform the duty deck officer who should confirm that the propeller is clear.

9 Electrical equipment

9.1 The risks of electric shock are much greater on board ship than they are normally ashore because the conditions of wetness, high humidity and high temperature (inducing sweating) reduce the contact resistance of the body. In those conditions, severe and even fatal shocks may be caused at voltages as low as 60V.

9.2 A notice of instructions on the treatment for electric shock should be posted in every space containing electrical equipment and switchgear. Immediate on the spot treatment of an unconscious patient is essential.

9.3 Before any work is done on electrical equipment, fuses should be removed or circuit breakers opened to ensure that all related circuits are dead. If possible, switches and circuit-breakers should be locked open or, alternatively, a 'not to be closed' notice attached (see 7.1). Where a fuse has been removed, it should be retained by the man working on the equipment until the job is finished. A check should be made that any interlocks or other safety devices are operative.

9.4 Flammable materials should never be left or stored near switchboards.

9.5 Carbon tetrachloride should not be used for cleaning electrical equipment because of the high toxicity of its vapours. Other safer cleaning solvents such as 1:1:1 trichloroethane are available but, even with these, the area of use should be well-ventilated. Solvents should always be used in accordance with manufacturers' instructions.

9.6 Work on or near live equipment should be avoided if possible but when it is essential for the safety of the ship or for testing purposes, the following precautions should be taken.

9.7 A second man, who should be competent in the treatment of electric shock, should be continually in attendance.

9.8 The working position adopted should be safe and secure to avoid possible fatal contact with live parts arising from a slip or stumble or the movement of the vessel. Insulated gloves should be worn where practicable.

9.9 Contact with the deck, particularly if it is wet, should be avoided. Footwear if damp or with metal studs or rivets may give inadequate insulation. The use of a dry insulating mat at all times is recommended.

9.10 Contact with bare metal should be avoided. A hand-to-hand shock is especially dangerous. To minimise the risk of a second contact should the working hand accidentally touch a live part, one hand should be kept in a trouser pocket whenever practicable.

9.11 Wrist watches, metal identity bracelets and rings should be removed. They provide low resistance contacts with the skin. Metal fittings on clothing and footwear are also dangerous.

9.12 Meter probes should have only minimum amounts of metal exposed and insulation of both probes should be in good condition. Care should be taken that the probes do not short circuit adjacent connections. In measuring voltages greater than 250V the probe should be attached and removed with the circuit dead.

10 Refrigeration machinery and refrigerated compartments

10.1 No one should enter a refrigerated chamber without first informing a responsible officer (see Chapter 20, section 4).

10.2 Personnel charging or repairing refrigeration plants should fully understand the precautions to be observed when handling the refrigerant.

10.3 Should it be known or suspected that the refrigerant has leaked into any compartment, no attempt should be made to enter that compartment without appropriate precautions being taken (see Chapter 10).

10.4 When refrigerant plants are being charged through a charging connection in the compressor suction line, it is sometimes the practice to heat the cylinder to evaporate the last of the liquid refrigerant. This should be done only by placing the cylinder in hot water or some similar indirect method and never by heating the cylinder directly with a blowlamp or other flame. Advice on the handling and storage of gas cylinders is given in Chapter 12, section 7.

10.5 When repair or maintenance necessitates the application of heat to vessels containing refrigerant, which form component parts of the refrigeration system, it should be ensured that appropriate valves are opened to prevent build-up of pressure within the vessels.

11 Steering gear

11.1 Generally, work should not be done on steering gear when a ship is under way. If it is necessary to work on steering gear when the vessel is at sea, the ship should be stopped and suitable steps taken to immobilise the rudder by closing the valves on the hydraulic cylinders or by other appropriate and effective means.

12 Hydraulic and pneumatic equipment

12.1 Before repairs to or maintenance of hydraulic and pneumatic equipment is undertaken, all pressure within the system should be released and the part being worked upon should be isolated from the power source. A warning notice should be displayed at the isolating valve.

12.2 Precautions should be taken against the possibility of residual pressure being released when unions or joints are broken.

12.3 Absolute cleanliness is essential to the proper and safe operation of hydraulic and pneumatic systems; the working area and tools, as well as the system and its components, should be kept clean during servicing work. Care should also be taken to ensure that replacement units are clean and free from any contamination, especially fluid passages.

12.4 Only those replacement components which comply with manufacturers' recommendations should be used.

12.5 Since vapours from hydraulic fluid may be flammable, naked lights should be kept away from hydraulic equipment being tested or serviced.

12.6 Any renewed or replacement item of equipment should be properly inspected or tested before being put into operation within the system.

12.7 A jet of hydraulic fluid under pressure should never be allowed to impinge upon the skin. Any hydraulic fluid spilt on the skin should be thoroughly washed off.

12.8 All equipment should be in a safe condition before the system is brought into operation.

CHAPTER 23

Servicing radio and associated electronic equipment

1 General

1.1 Exposure to dangerous levels of microwave radiation should be avoided by strict adherence to instructions about special precautions contained in manufacturers' handbooks. Radar sets should not be operated with wave guides disconnected unless it is necessary for servicing purposes, when special precautions should be taken.

1.2 Work should not be undertaken within the marked safety radius of Satellite Terminal Antennae unless its transmitter has been rendered inoperative.

1.3 Eyes are particularly vulnerable to microwave and ultra-violet radiation. Care should be taken to avoid looking directly into a radar aerial or waveguide while it is in operation or where arcing or sparking is likely to occur.

1.4 Exposure to dangerous levels of X-ray radiation may occur in the vicinity of faulty high voltage valves. Care should be exercised when fault tracing in the modulator circuits of radar equipment. An open circuited heater of such valves can lead to X-ray radiation where the anode voltage is in excess of 5000V.

1.5 Vapours of some solvents used for degreasing are toxic, particularly carbon tetrachloride which should never be used. Great care should be exercised when using solvents particularly in confined spaces; there should be no smoking. Manufacturers' instructions should be followed.

1.6 Some dry recorder papers used in echo sounders and facsimile recorders give off toxic fumes in use. The equipment should be well-ventilated to avoid inhalation of the fumes.

1.7 Radio transmitters and radar equipment should not be operated when men are working in the vicinity of aerials; the equipment should be isolated from mains supply and radio transmitters earthed. When equipment has been isolated, warning notices should be placed on transmitting and radar equipment and at the mains supply point, to prevent apparatus being switched on until clearance has been received from those concerned that they have finished the outside work.

1.8 Aerials should be rigged out of reach of persons standing at normal deck level or mounting easily accessible parts of the superstructure. If that is impracticable, safety screens should be erected.

1.9 Notices warning of the danger of high voltage should be displayed near radio transmitter aerials and lead-through insulators.

2 Electrical hazards

2.1 Conditions on board ship often create greater than normal risks of electric shock (see Chapter 22, section 9). It should also be borne in mind that cuts and abrasions significantly reduce skin resistance.

2.2 Fuses should be removed from equipment before work is begun, and retained while the work is proceeding.

2.3 Where accumulators are used they should be disconnected at source; otherwise precautions should be taken to avoid short circuiting the accumulator terminals with consequent risk of burns.

2.4 Live chassis connected to one side of the mains are usually marked appropriately and should be handled with caution. Where the mains are AC and a transformer is interposed, the chassis is usually connected to the earth side of the supply, but this should be verified using an appropriate meter.

2.5 When some types of equipment are switched off but the mains switches are left on, some parts may remain live; power should always be cut off at the mains.

2.6 Modern equipment often embodies a master crystal enclosed in an oven; the supply to the oven is taken from an independent source and is not disconnected when the transmitter is switched off and the mains switch is off. Mains voltage will be present inside the transmitter, and care should be taken.

2.7 Before work is begun on the EHT section of a transmitter or other HT apparatus, with the mains switched off, all HT capacitors should be discharged using an insulated jumper, inserting a resistor in the circuit to slow the rate of discharge. This precaution should be taken even where the capacitors have permanent discharge resistors fitted.

2.8 An electrolytic capacitor that is suspect, or shows blistering, should be replaced, since it is liable to explode when electrical supply is on. There is a similar risk when an electrolytic capacitor is discharged by a short circuit.

2.9 Work at or near live equipment should be avoided if possible but where it is essential for the safety of the ship or for testing purposes then the additional precautions described in Chapter 22, section 9.6–12 should be taken.

3 Valves and semi-conductor devices

3.1 Valves being removed from equipment which has recently been operating should be grasped with a heat resistant cloth; in case of large valves, eg power amplifier, OP and modulators, which reach a high temperature in operation, cooling down time should be allowed before they are removed. Severe burns can result if they touch bare skin.

3.2 Cathode ray tubes and large thermionic valves should be handled with care; although they implode when broken, there is still a risk of severe cuts from sharp-edged glass fragments. Some special purpose devices contain vapour or gas at high pressure, for example Trigatron, but these are usually covered with a protective fibre network to contain the glass should they explode.

3.3 Beryllia (beryllium oxide) dust is very dangerous if inhaled or if it penetrates the skin through a cut or abrasion. It may be present in some electronic components. Cathode ray tubes, power transistors, diodes and thyristors containing it will be usually identified by the manufacturers' information provided, but lack of such information should not be taken as a positive indication of its absence. Those heat sink washers which contain it are highly polished and look like dark brass. These items should be carefully stored in their original packings until required.

3.4 Physical damage to components of this kind whether they are new or defective is likely to produce dangerous dust; abrasion should be avoided, they should not be worked by tools and encapsulations should be left intact. Excessive heat can be dangerous, but normal soldering with thermal shunt is safe. Damaged or broken parts should be separately and securely packed, following the manufacturer's instructions for return or disposal.

3.5 Persons handling parts containing beryllia should wear protective clothing, including gloves, to prevent beryllia coming into contact with the skin. Tweezers should be used where practicable. If the skin does become contaminated with the dust, affected parts, particularly any cuts, should be cleaned without delay.

4 Work on apparatus on extension runners or on the bench

4.1 Chassis on extension runners should be firmly fixed, either by self-locking devices or by use of chocks, before any work is done.

4.2 Where units are awkward or heavy for one person to handle easily, assistance should be sought (see Chapter 11). Strain, rupture or a slipped disc can result from a lone effort.

4.3 Any chassis on the bench should be firmly wedged or otherwise secured to prevent it overbalancing or moving. Should a live chassis overbalance, no attempt should be made to grab it.

4.4 Sharp edges and tag connectors on a chassis can cause cuts. Should the tag be alive and the skin is pierced, the shock experienced will be out of proportion to the voltage.

4.5 Temporary connections should be soundly made. Flexible extension cables should have good insulation and adequate current carrying capacity.

CHAPTER 24

Storage batteries

1 General

1.1 When a battery is being charged it 'gases', giving off both hydrogen and oxygen. Because hydrogen is easily ignited in concentrations ranging from 4 per cent to 75 per cent in air, battery containers and compartments should be kept adequately ventilated to prevent an accumulation of dangerous gas.

1.2 Smoking and any type of open flame should be prohibited in a battery compartment. A conspicuous notice to this effect should be displayed at the entrance to the compartment.

1.3 Lighting fittings in battery compartments should be properly maintained at all times, with protective glasses in position and properly tightened. If cracked or broken glasses cannot be replaced immediately, the electric circuit should be isolated until replacements are obtained.

1.4 No unauthorised modifications or additions should be made to electrical equipment (including lighting fittings) in battery compartments.

1.5 Portable electric lamps and tools, and other portable power tools which might give rise to sparks should not be used in battery compartments.

1.6 The battery compartment should not be used as a store for any materials or gear not associated with the batteries.

1.7 A short circuit of even one cell may produce an arc or sparks which may cause an explosion of any hydrogen present. Additionally, the very heavy current which can flow in the short circuiting wire or tool may cause burns due to rapid overheating of the metal.

1.8 Insulation and/or guarding of cables in battery compartments should be maintained in good condition.

1.9 All battery connections should be kept clean and tight to avoid sparking and overheating. Temporary clip-on connections should never be used as they may work loose due to vibration and cause a spark or short circuit.

1.10 Metal tools, such as wrenches and spanners, should never be placed on top of batteries as they may cause sparks or short circuits. The use of insulated tools is recommended.

1.11 Jewellery, watches and rings etc should be removed when working on batteries. A short circuit through any of these items will heat it rapidly and may cause a severe skin burn. If rings cannot be removed, they should be heavily taped in insulating material.

1.12 All circuits fed by the battery should be switched off when leads are being connected or disconnected. If a battery is in sections, it may be possible to reduce the voltage between cells in the work area, and hence the severity of an accidental short circuit or electric shock, by removing the jumper leads between sections before work is begun. It should be appreciated that whilst individual cell voltages may not present a shock risk, dangerous voltages can exist where numbers of cells are connected together in series. A lethal shock needs a current of only a few tens of milliamps and particular care should be exercised where the voltage exceeds 50V.

1.13 Battery cell vent plugs should be screwed tight while connections are being made or broken.

1.14 The ventilation tubes of battery boxes should be examined regularly to ensure that they are free from obstruction.

1.15 Lids of battery boxes should be fastened while open for servicing and properly secured again when the work is finished.

1.16 Batteries should be kept battened in position to prevent shifting in rough weather.

1.17 Alkaline and lead-acid batteries should be kept in separate compartments. Where both lead-acid and alkaline batteries are in use, great care should be exercised to keep apart the materials and tools used in servicing each type, as contamination of the electrolyte may cause deterioration of battery performance and mixing of the two electrolytes produces a vigorous chemical reaction which could be very dangerous.

1.18 Both acid and alkaline electrolytes are highly corrosive. Immediate remedial action should be taken to wash off any accidental splashes on the person or on equipment. Hands should always be washed as soon as the work has finished.

1.19 Batteries should always be transported in the upright position to avoid spillage of electrolyte. A sufficient number of men should be employed since the batteries are heavy and painful strains or injury can otherwise easily result (see Chapter 11).

2 Lead-acid batteries

2.1 When the electrolyte is being prepared, the concentrated sulphuric acid should be added SLOWLY to the water. IF WATER IS ADDED TO THE ACID, THE HEAT GENERATED MAY CAUSE AN EXPLOSION OF STEAM, SPATTERING ACID OVER THE PERSON HANDLING IT.

2.2 Goggles, rubber gloves and protective apron should be worn when acid is handled.

2.3 To neutralise acid on skin or clothes, copious quantities of clean fresh water should be used.

2.4 An eyewash bottle should be to hand in the compartment for immediate use on the eyes in case of accident. This bottle should be clearly distinguishable by touch from acid or other containers, so that it may be easily located by a person who is temporarily blinded.

2.5 The corrosion products which form round the terminals of batteries are injurious to skin and eyes. They should be removed by brushing, away from the body. Terminals should be protected with petroleum jelly.

2.6 An excessive charging rate causes acid mist to be carried out of the vents onto adjacent surfaces. This should be cleaned off with diluted ammonia water or soda solution, and affected areas then dried.

3 Alkaline batteries

3.1 The general safety precautions with this type of battery are the same as for the lead-acid batteries with the following exceptions.

3.2 The electrolyte in these batteries is alkaline but is similarly corrosive. It should not be allowed to come into contact with the skin or clothing. In the case of contact with the skin, the affected parts should be washed with copious quantities of clean fresh water, but if burns ensue, boracic powder or a saturated solution of boracic powder should be applied. Eyes should be washed out thoroughly with plenty of clean fresh water followed immediately with a solution of boracic powder (at the rate of one teaspoonful to ½ litre or 1 pint of water). This solution should be always readily accessible when the electrolyte is handled.

3.3 Unlike lead-acid batteries, metal cases of alkaline batteries remain live at all times and care should be taken not to touch them or to allow metal tools to come into contact with them.

CHAPTER 25

Work in galley, pantry and other food handling areas

1 Health and hygiene

1.1 Catering staff have a responsibility for ensuring that high standards of personal hygiene and cleanliness of the galley, pantry and mess rooms are always maintained.

1.2 Hands and fingernails should be washed and cleaned before food is handled. This is most important after visiting the toilet.

1.3 All cuts, however small, should be reported immediately and receive first aid attention to prevent infection.

1.4 An open cut, burn or abrasion should be covered with a waterproof dressing.

1.5 Illness, rashes or spots should be reported immediately the symptoms appear.

1.6 A person suffering from dysentery or diarrhoea should not work in the galley, pantry or other food handling areas.

1.7 Catering staff should wear clean clothing when handling food and preparing meals. A supply of clean, hot, running water, clean towels and soap should be available.

1.8 Cleanliness of all food, crockery, cutlery, linen, utensils, equipment and storage is vital. Cracked or chipped crockery and glassware should be destroyed.

1.9 Foodstuffs which may have come into contact with broken glass or broken crockery should be thrown away.

1.10 There should be no smoking in galleys, pantries, store rooms or other places where food is prepared.

1.11 Crockery and glassware should not be left submerged in washing up water where it may easily be broken and cause injury. Such items should be washed up individually as should knives and any utensils or implements with sharp edges.

1.12 Some domestic cleaning substances, for example caustic soda and bleaches, can burn the skin. They may also react dangerously if mixed together (see also Chapter 1, section 2).

2 Slips, falls and tripping hazards

2.1 A large proportion of injuries to catering staff arise from slips and falls caused by wearing unsuitable footwear; 'flip-flops', sandals, plimsolls etc are especially dangerous on greasy decks and they afford no protection to the feet from burns or scalds if hot or boiling liquids are spilt. Suitable footwear, preferably with slip-resistant soles, should be worn at all times.

2.2 Decks and gratings should be kept free of grease, rubbish and ice etc to obviate slipping which may result in serious injuries especially when hot liquids or glass and crockery are being carried. Any spillage should be cleared up immediately.

2.3 Broken glass or crockery should be cleared away with a brush and pan – never with bare hands.

2.4 The area of deck immediately outside the entrance to refrigerated rooms should have an anti-slip surface.

2.5 Care should be taken when using stairs and companionways; one hand should always be kept free to grasp the handrail.

2.6 Trays, crates, cartons etc should not be carried in such fashion that sills, storm steps or other obstructions in the path are obscured from view.

3 Galley stoves and steam boilers

3.1 Care should be taken in lighting oil-fired galley stoves. The following procedures should always be adopted:

(a) the inside of the furnace should be checked to see that there is no oil in it and air should be blown through to clear any oil vapour; a blowback may occur if an attempt is made to light the burner with oil or oil vapour in the furnace;

(b) the oil should be at the correct temperature for the grade of oil being used; if not, the temperature of the oil should be regulated before lighting is attempted;

(c) the torch specially provided for the purpose should always be used for lighting a burner; other means of ignition, eg by the introduction of loose burning material into the stove, should not be used. An attempt to relight a burner from the hot brickwork of the stove may result in an explosion;

(d) if all is in order, the operator should stand to one side, the lighted torch should be inserted and the fuel turned on. Care should be taken that there is not too much oil on the torch, which could drip and possibly cause a fire;

(e) if the oil does not light immediately, the fuel supply should be turned off and the furnace ventilated by allowing air to blow through for two or three minutes to clear any oil vapour before a second attempt to light. During this interval, the burner should be removed and the atomiser and tip inspected to verify that they are in good order;

(f) if while the burner is alight there is a total flame failure in the furnace the fuel supply should be completely closed off.

3.2 Catering staff should not attempt to repair electric or oil-fired ranges. Defects should always be reported so that proper repairs may be made. The equipment should be taken out of use until repaired.

3.3 The indiscriminate use of water in hosing down and washing equipment in the galley can be very dangerous, particularly where there are electrical installations. Whenever the galley deck is washed down, power to an electric range and all electric equipment should be switched off and isolated from the supply and water kept from contact with the electrical equipment.

3.4 Range guard rails should be used in rough weather. Pots and pans should never be filled to the extent that the contents slop over when the ship rolls.

3.5 Dry cloths or pot holders should always be used to handle hot pans and dishes. Wet cloths conduct heat quickly and may scald the hands.

3.6 No one should be directly in front of an oven when the door is opened – the initial heat blast can cause burns.

3.7 The steam supply to pressure cookers, steamers and boilers should be turned off and pressure released before their lids are opened.

3.8 Fat should not be rendered down in ovens. If forgotten, it may overheat and catch fire. A thermostatically-controlled frier may be used for the purpose but fat is best rendered down with a little water in a deep heavy-bottomed pot.

3.9 Water should never be poured into hot fat; the water turns into steam, throwing the fat considerable distances. This may cause severe burns to personnel, and possibly start a fire.

3.10 If fat catches fire in a container, the flames should be smothered if practicable and the container removed from the source of heat. Otherwise a suitable fire extinguisher should be used. In no circumstances should water be used.

4 Catering equipment

4.1 Except under the supervision of an experienced person, no one should use catering equipment unless trained in its use and fully instructed in the precautions to be observed.

4.2 Dangerous parts of catering machines should be properly guarded and the guards kept in position whenever the machine is in use.

4.3 Any machine or equipment that is defective in its parts, guards or safety devices should be reported and taken out of service, with power disconnected, until repaired.

4.4 When a power-operated machine has to be cleaned or a blockage in it removed, it should be switched off and isolated from the power supply. Some machines will continue to run down for a while thereafter, and care should be taken to see that dangerous parts have come to rest before cleaning is begun.

4.5 A safe procedure for cleaning all machines should be established and carefully followed. Every precaution should be taken when cutting edges, for example on slicing machines, are exposed by the necessary removal of guards to allow thorough cleaning. Guards should be properly and securely replaced immediately the job is done.

4.6 Unless properly supervised, a person under eighteen years of age should not clean any power operated or manually driven machine with dangerous parts which may move during the cleaning operation.

4.7 Appropriate implements, not fingers, should be used to feed materials into processing machines.

4.8 Electrical equipment should not be used with wet hands.

5 Knives, saws, choppers etc

5.1 Sharp implements should be treated with respect and handled with care at all times. They should not be left lying around working areas where someone may accidentally cut themselves. They should not be mixed in with other items for washing up but cleaned individually and should be stored in a safe place.

5.2 Knives should be kept tidily in a drawer or rack when not in use.

5.3 The handles of knives, saws, choppers etc should be securely fixed and kept clean and free from grease. The cutting edges should be kept clean and sharp.

5.4 Proper can openers should be used to open cans; improvisations are dangerous and may leave jagged edges on the can.

5.5 Chopping meat requires undivided attention. The chopping block must be firm, the cutting area of the meat well on the block and hands and body clear of the line of strike. There must be adequate room for movement and no obstructions in the way of the cutting stroke. Particular care is required when the vessel is moving in a seaway.

5.6 Foodstuffs being chopped with a knife should not be fed towards the blade with outstretched fingers. Finger tips should be bent inwards towards the palm of the hand with the thumb overlapped by the forefinger. The knife blade should be angled away from the work and so away from the fingers.

5.7 A falling knife should be left to fall, not grabbed.

5.8 A meat saw should be guided by the forefinger of the free hand over the top of the blade. The use of firm even strokes will allow the blade to feel its way; if forced, the saw may jump possibly causing injury.

6 Refrigerated rooms and store rooms

6.1 All refrigerated room doors should be fitted with means both of opening the door and of sounding an alarm from the inside.

6.2 A routine testing of the alarm bell and checking of the door clasps and inside release should be carried out regularly, at least at weekly intervals.

6.3 Those using the refrigerated room should make themselves familiar with the operation, in darkness, of the inside release for the door and the location of the alarm button.

6.4 All refrigerated room doors should be fitted with an arrangement of adequate strength to hold the door open in a seaway and should be secured open while stores are being handled. These doors are extremely heavy and can cause serious injury to a person caught between the door and the jamb.

6.5 Anyone going into a refrigerated room should take the padlock, if any, inside with him. Another person should be informed.

6.6 Cold stores or refrigerated rooms should not be entered if it is suspected that there has been a leakage of refrigerant. A warning notice to this effect should be posted outside the doors.

6.7 All stores and crates should be stowed securely so they do not shift or move in a seaway.

6.8 When wooden boxes or crates are opened, protruding fastenings should be removed or made safe.

6.9 Where a metal strip secures the lid of a tea chest it should be completely removed or made safe, otherwise its jagged edge may cause injury.

6.10 Meat hooks not in use should be stowed in a special container provided for the purpose. Where hooks cannot be removed they should be kept clear.

CHAPTER 26

Work in ships' laundries

1 General

1.1 Many of the general hazards found in the ship's laundry are similar to those elsewhere on the ship; strains can be caused by improper handling of awkward or heavy loads, equipment and washing left in gangways can cause falls and defective or improperly used machinery can cause injuries. There are also specific hazards in laundries which require particular attention.

1.2 Floors in laundry spaces can become extremely slippery when wet, especially where soap solutions are used. Constant care is needed and suitable footwear should be worn (see Chapter 5, section 6 and Chapter 9, sections 1, 2 and 7).

2 Burns and scalds

2.1 Many accidents in laundries involve scalding by steam or hot liquids or burns from hot surfaces. Every hot vessel or machine and every container of scalding liquid should be regarded as a potential danger, capable of causing injury and adequate precautions should be taken.

2.2 Good ventilation should be maintained to reduce heat and humidity in the working environment.

2.3 Where high pressure steam is used to heat water, the supply pressure should be regulated to ensure excessive steam cannot be applied to any machine.

3 Machinery and equipment

3.1 All personnel required to work in the laundry or use any part of the equipment there should be fully instructed on the proper operation of the machinery. A person under 18 years of age should not work on industrial washing machines, hydro-extractors, calenders or garment presses unless he is fully instructed as to precautions to be observed, and has received sufficient training in work at the machine or is under close supervision by a suitably experienced person.

3.2 Equipment should be inspected before use for faults and damage. Particular attention should be paid to the automatic cut-off or interlocking arrangements on washing machines, hydro-extractors etc and the guards and emergency stops on presses, calenders, mangling and wringing machines. Any defect or irregularity found during inspection, or apparent during operation of the equipment, should be reported immediately and the use of the machine discontinued until such time as any necessary repairs or adjustments have been carried out. A notice warning against use should be displayed prominently on the defective machine.

3.3 Frequent and regular inspection and thorough checking of all electrical equipment and apparatus are also necessary to ensure the standard of maintenance essential under the conditions which prevail in laundries.

3.4 Machines should not be overloaded and loads should be distributed uniformly.

3.5 Reliance should not be placed entirely on interlocking or cut-off arrangements on the doors of washing machines, hydro-extractors and drying tumblers etc; doors should not be opened until all movement has ceased.

4 Dry-cleaning operations

4.1 The principal hazard presented by a dry-cleaning solvent is that it is highly volatile, producing a vapour which is anaesthetic. The vapour is capable of inducing drowsiness, followed by unconsciousness and eventually death if the concentration is high enough and the affected person is not quickly removed to fresh air. Effective mechanical ventilation should therefore be provided in any compartment containing dry-cleaning plant. The purpose of such ventilation is to ensure that the vapour concentration never exceeds the 'threshold limit value' which is the airborne concentration of vapour to which it is believed that nearly all persons may be repeatedly exposed without adverse effects.

4.2 Another hazard is that the vapour, if allowed to contact naked flames or red-hot surfaces, decomposes into toxic and corrosive substances which are dangers to health. Smoking should therefore be prohibited in compartments where the solvent is present.

4.3 The vapour is heavier than air, and may therefore build up in the bottom of a compartment.

4.4 Dry cleaning solvent is also a potential cause of de-fatting of the skin, which may lead to cracking of the skin with the resultant possibility of infection from other sources. Suitable impermeable, cotton-lined PVC gloves should therefore be worn when handling it.

4.5 An officer should be appointed to take overall responsibility for the security and operation of the dry-cleaning plant. The responsible officer should ensure that the plant compartment is locked at all times when the plant is not in use, and that only the operator and himself normally has access to it.

4.6 The responsible officer should be satisfied that the plant operator is fully aware of:

(a) the operating and maintenance procedures as laid down in the manufacturer's instruction manual, a copy of which should be kept on board the ship;

(b) action necessary in the event of malfunctions of the plant, in the interests of personal safety;

(c) the precautions to be taken in handling the solvent, and dealing with spillages;

(d) the inherent dangers of excessive concentrations of solvent vapour;

(e) the meaning of cautionary notices displayed in the plant compartment.

Appropriate protective clothing should be made available, and a second person should be present in case of emergency.

4.7 Warning notices appropriate to the particular solvent used should be displayed prominently and permanently in the plant compartment. Such notices should be obtained from the solvent manufacturer, and should include instructions in first aid for persons overcome by solvent vapour.

4.8 Where separate compartments are provided for the storage of solvent, the same general precautions as above should be observed, including the provision of suitable warning notices and the instructions in first aid.

4.9 Solvent being transferred manually from the store to the plant compartment should be carried in a closed container.

4.10 Thick and padded articles, such as sleeping bags and quilts, should not be dry-cleaned. They are very retentive of the dry-cleaning solvent from which it is extremely difficult to free them, and body warmth when the articles are put into use again is likely to cause vapours to be emitted from the trapped residues.

4.11 Articles which have been dry-cleaned should be aired very thoroughly on the ventilated rack provided, to remove any solvent fumes.

5 Fire prevention

5.1 Hand pressing irons should not be left standing on materials likely to be combustible.

5.2 Clothing should be left to dry only in the designated places. It should not be put to dry in any machinery space or on or close to electric heaters, radiators, etc in accommodation spaces.

CHAPTER 27

General cargo ships

Note: Chapters 11, 17, 18 and 19 have special relevance to work on general cargo ships.

1 Stowage of cargo

1.1 Cargo should be stowed in 'tween decks with due regard to the order of discharging, so that when beams and hatches have to be removed with cargo remaining in the 'tween deck, there will be a space of at least 1 metre (39 inches) between the hatch coaming and the cargo at the sides and ends of the hatchway or section of hatchway to be worked. Guidelines should be painted on 'tween decks on all sides of the hatch coamings.

1.2 Wherever practicable, cargo should be stowed so as to leave safe clearance behind the rungs of hold ladders and to allow safe access as may be necessary at sea.

1.3 Deck cargo should be stowed in accordance with the relevant provisions of the *Merchant Shipping* (*Load Line*) (*Deck Cargo*) *Regulations 1968*, clear of hatch coamings to leave safe access for seamen. Obstructions in the access way such as lashings or securing points should be painted white to make them more easily visible. Where this is impracticable and cargo is stowed against ships' rails or hatch coamings to such a height that the rails or coamings do not give effective protection to the crew from falling overboard or into the open hold, temporary fencing should be provided (see Chapter 9, section 5).

1.4 When deck cargo is stowed against and above ships' rails or bulwarks, a wire rope pendant or a chain, extending from the ring bolts or other anchorage on the deck to the full height of the deck cargo, should be provided to obviate seamen having to go overside to attach derrick guys and preventers directly to the anchorages on the deck.

1.5 Where hatches will have to be opened at intermediate ports before deck cargo is unloaded, it should be stowed leaving a clear space of at least 1 metre (39 inches) around the coamings or around the part of the hatch that is to be opened. If this is impracticable, provision should be made by fencing or life-lines, to enable seamen to remove and replace beams and hatch coverings in safety.

2 Dangerous goods and substances

2.1 Regulations concerning the carriage of dangerous substances are contained in the current Merchant Shipping (Dangerous Goods) Rules (and any amending Rules), reproduced in the current edition of the *Report of the Department of Trade Standing Advisory Committee on the Carriage of Dangerous Goods in Ships* (the 'Blue Book'). The 'Blue Book' together with the *International Maritime Dangerous Goods Code* (IMDG Code) lists many substances regarded as dangerous and recommends how they should be classified, packed, labelled and stowed in order to comply with the Rules.

2.2 The general introduction and the introductions to individual classes of both the 'Blue Book' and the IMDG Code contain many provisions to ensure the safe handling and carriage of dangerous goods including requirements for electrical equipment and wiring, fire fighting equipment, ventilation, smoking, repair work, provision and availability of special equipment etc, some of which are general for all classes and others particular to certain classes only. It is important that reference should be made to this information before handling dangerous goods. Some of the requirements are highlighted in subsequent paragraphs. Where any doubts exist, advice should be sought from the Department of Trade or other competent authority.

2.3 Dangerous substances should be loaded or unloaded only under the supervision of a responsible officer.

2.4 Dangerous substances should not be loaded unless they have been packed and labelled in compliance with the 'Blue Book' or

IMDG Code. In the case of dangerous substances shipped in bulk, where labelling may not be required, their identity and the hazards to which they give rise should be checked against the dangerous cargo booking list.

2.5 When seamen are required to handle consignments containing dangerous substances, adequate information should be available as to the nature of such substances and any special precautions to be observed. In the event of accidental exposure to dangerous substances, reference should be made to the IMDG Medical Guide for remedial action.

2.6 Suitable precautions, such as the provision of special lifting gear, should be taken to prevent damage to receptacles containing dangerous substances.

2.7 In compartments containing cargo having an explosion or fire risk (for example, explosives and flammable liquids), all electrical circuits and equipment should meet the recommendations of the 'Blue Book'. When loading or unloading such cargo, firefighting equipment should be rigged ready for immediate use. Smoking should be prohibited while cargo handling is in progress, except in authorised places.

2.8 Where necessary, seamen loading, unloading or otherwise handling dangerous substances should wear appropriate protective clothing and personal protective equipment, including respiratory equipment (see Chapter 5).

2.9 Appropriate measures should be taken promptly to render harmless any spillage of dangerous substances. Particular care should be taken when dangerous substances are carried in refrigerated spaces where any spillage may be absorbed by the insulating material. Insulation affected in this way should be inspected and renewed if necessary.

2.10 Where there is leakage or escape of dangerous gases or vapours from the cargo, seamen should leave the danger area. The area should be ventilated and tested, if possible, to verify that the concentration of gases or vapours in the atmosphere is not high enough to be dangerous, before personnel are allowed to enter the area again. Seamen required to deal with spillages or to remove defective packages should be provided with and wear suitable breathing apparatus and protective clothing as the circumstances dictate. Suitable rescue and resuscitation equipment should be readily available in case of an emergency (see Chapter 10).

3 Working cargo

3.1 No other work such as chipping, caulking, spray painting, shotblasting or welding etc, should be carried out in a space where cargo working is in progress if it thereby gives rise to a hazard to persons working in the space.

3.2 Loads being lowered or hoisted should not pass or remain over any person engaged in loading or unloading or performing other work in the vicinity.

3.3 Care should be taken when using ladders in the square of the hatch while cargo is being worked.

3.4 A signaller should always be employed at a hatchway when cargo is being loaded or discharged unless the crane driver or winchman has a complete unrestricted view of the load. The signals set out in Chapter 17 should be used.

3.5 The signaller should be in a position where he can best follow the work and be seen by the winchman; his view should be clear and unobstructed.

3.6 Before giving a signal to hoist, the signaller should receive clearance from the person making up the load that it is secure, and should ascertain that no one else would be endangered by the hoist. Before giving the signal to lower, he should warn persons in the way and ensure all are clear.

3.7 When a load does not ride properly after being hoisted, the signaller should immediately give warning of danger and the load should be lowered and adjusted as necessary.

3.8 Hooks, slings and other gear should not be loaded beyond their safe working loads.

3.9 Loads should be raised and lowered smoothly, avoiding sudden jerks or 'snatching' loads.

3.10 Strops and slings should be of sufficient size and length to enable them to be used safely and be so applied and pulled sufficiently tight to prevent the load or any part of the load from slipping and falling.

3.11 Loads (sets) should be properly put together and properly slung before they are hoisted or lowered.

3.12 Before heavy loads such as long lengths of steel sections, tubes, lumber, etc are swung, the load should be given a trial lift in order to test the efficacy of the slinging.

3.13 Except for the purpose of breaking out or making up slings, lifting hooks should not be attached to:

(a) the bands, strops or other fastenings of packages of cargo, unless these fastenings have been specifically provided for lifting purposes;

(b) the rims (chines) of barrels or drums for lifting purposes, unless the construction and condition of the barrels or drums is such as to permit lifting to be done safely with properly designed and constructed can hooks.

3.14 Suitable precautions, such as the use of packing or chafing pieces, should be taken to prevent chains, wire and fibre ropes from being damaged by the sharp edges of loads.

3.15 When slings are used with barrel hooks or similar holding devices where the weight of the load holds the hooks in place, the sling should be led down through the egg or eye link and through the eye of each hook in turn so that the horizontal part of the sling draws the hooks together.

3.16 The angle between the legs of slings should not normally exceed 90°. Where this is not reasonably practicable, the angle may be extended up to 120° provided that the slings have been designed to work at the greater angles.

3.17 Trays and pallets should be hoisted with four-legged slings and where necessary nets or other means should be used to prevent any part of the load falling.

3.18 When bundles of long metal goods such as tubes, pipes and rails are being hoisted, two slings should be used and, where necessary, a spreader. A suitable lanyard should also be attached, where necessary.

3.19 Wire rope slings of adequate size should be used for loading and discharging logs; tongs should not be used except to break out loads.

3.20 Cargo buckets, tubs and similar appliances should be carefully filled so that there is no risk of the contents falling out and be securely attached to the hoist (for example, by a shackle) to prevent tipping and displacement during hoisting and lowering.

3.21 Shackles should be used for slinging thick sheet metal, if there are suitable holes in the material; otherwise suitable clamps on an endless sling should be used.

3.22 Bricks and other loose goods of similar shape, carboys, small drums, canisters, etc should be loaded or discharged in suitable boxes or pallets with sufficiently high sides, lifted by four-legged slings.

3.23 Slings or chains being returned to the loading position should be securely hooked on the cargo hook before the signaller gives the signal to hoist. Hooks or claws should be attached to the egg link or shackle of the cargo hook, not allowed to hang loose. The cargo hook should be kept high enough to keep slings or chains clear of persons and obstructions.

3.24 When work is interrupted or has ceased for the time being, the hatch should be left in a safe condition, with either guard rails or the hatch covers in position.

CHAPTER 28

Carriage of containers

1 To the extent that containers are simply large packages of pre-stowed cargo, many of the provisions of Chapters 17, 18, 19 and 27 are relevant to the safe working of containers.

2 A container may hold dangerous goods. Before loading begins, the dangerous cargo booking list should be scrutinised to ensure that the containers (which should be appropriately marked) may be correctly stowed.

3 In handling containers, care should be taken against the possibility of uneven loading and poor distribution of weight of the contents.

4 Containers carried on deck should be properly secured in such a manner as to take account of the appropriate strength features of the container and the stresses caused by the stacking of one or more upon the other.

5 Heavy items of machinery or plant and bagged bulk products which are stored on flats, may need to be further secured by additional lashings.

6 On ships not specially constructed or adapted for their carriage, containers should, whenever possible, be stowed fore and aft and should be securely lashed. Containers should not be stowed over hatches unless it is known that the hatches are of the requisite overall and point load-bearing strength.

7 Safe means should be provided for access to the top of a container to check lashings etc. Persons so engaged should, where appropriate, be protected from falling by use of a safety harness properly secured or by other suitable arrangements.

8 Deck lashing points which obtrude on walkways should be painted white, and warning notices displayed.

CHAPTER 29

Tankers and bulk product carriers

1 General

1.1 Personnel joining a tanker or similar vessel for the first time should receive a basic safety induction to the main hazards associated with the vessel, either before or on joining the ship.

1.2 Training in emergency procedures and in the use of any special emergency equipment should be given as appropriate to members of the crew at regular intervals. The instruction should include personal first aid measures for dealing with accidental contact with harmful substances in the cargo being carried and inhalation of dangerous gases or fumes.

1.3 Because of the risks of ill effects from contamination by cargoes carried in these ships, especially chemical tankers and carriers, personnel should maintain very high standards of personal cleanliness and particularly so when they have been engaged in cargo handling or tank cleaning. Hands should be thoroughly washed before breaks for smoking or meals. Shower baths and changes of clothing after each duty period are advisable. Dirty clothing should not be stowed in cabins.

1.4 Only 'certified safe' electrical equipment of approved design should be allowed in the cargo areas. The safety of this equipment depends on maintenance of a high order which should be carried out only by competent persons. Unauthorised personnel should not interfere with such equipment. Any faults observed, such as loose or missing fastenings or covers, severe corrosion, cracked or broken lamp glasses etc should be reported immediately.

2 Oil and bulk ore/oil carriers

2.1 Tankers and other ships carrying petroleum or petroleum products in bulk, or in ballast after carrying those cargoes, are at risk from fire or explosion arising from ignition of vapours from the cargo which may in some circumstances penetrate into any part of the ship.

2.2 Additionally, vapours may be toxic, some in very low concentrations, and some liquid products, especially petrol (gasoline) treated with tetra-ethyl or tetra-methyl-lead, are harmful in contact with the skin.

2.3 Guidance on the general precautions which should be taken is given in publications of the International Chamber of Shipping:

(a) *International Safety Guide for Oil Tankers and Terminals*

(b) *Safety in Oil Tankers, a handbook for crew members.*

Companies may additionally issue their own safety regulations. These publications should be available on board and the guidance conscientiously followed.

2.4 Those on board responsible for the safe loading and carriage of the cargo should have all relevant information about its nature and character before it is loaded and about the precautions which need to be observed during the voyage. The remainder of the crew should be advised of any precautions which they too should observe.

2.5 High fire risks require the strict observance of rules restricting smoking and the carriage of matches or cigarette lighters.

2.6 Spillages and leakages of cargo should be attended to promptly. Oil-soaked rags should not be discarded carelessly where they may be a fire hazard or possibly ignite spontaneously. Other combustible rubbish should not be allowed to accumulate.

2.7 Cargo handling equipment, testing instruments, automatic and other alarm systems and personal protective equipment should be maintained to a very high standard of efficiency at all times.

2.8 Work about the ship which might cause sparking or which involves heat should not be undertaken unless authorised after the work area has been tested and found gas-free, or its safety is otherwise assured.

2.9 Where any enclosed space has to be entered, the precautions given in Chapter 10 should be strictly observed. Dangerous gases may be released or leak from adjoining spaces while work is in progress and frequent testing of the atmosphere should be undertaken.

2.10 'Permit-to-work' procedures should be adopted unless the work to be carried out presents no undue hazard (see Chapter 7).

3 Liquefied gas carriers

3.1 Guidance on the general precautions which should be taken on these vessels is given in the *Tanker Safety Guide* (*Liquefied Gas*) published by the International Chamber of Shipping and in the publications mentioned in section 2.3. The IMCO recommended *Code for the Construction and Equipment of Ships Carrying Liquefied Gas in Bulk* also contains guidance on operational needs. These publications should be available on board liquefied gas carriers together with any special safety regulations issued by the company.

3.2 The provisions in paras 2.4 to 2.10 of the preceding section also apply.

3.3 In addition, it should be noted that cargo pipes, valves and connections and any point of leakage of the gas cargo may be intensely cold. Contact may cause severe cold burns.

3.4 Pressure should be carefully reduced and liquid cargo drained from any part of the cargo transfer system, including discharge lines, before any opening up or disconnecting is begun.

3.5 Some cargoes such as ammonia have a very pungent, suffocating odour that even in very small quantities may cause eye irritation and disorientation together with chemical burns. Seafarers should take this into account when moving about the vessel, and especially when climbing ladders and gangways. The means of access to the vessel should be such that it can be closely supervised and is sited as far away from the manifold area as possible. Crew members should be aware of the location of eye wash and safety showers.

4 Chemical carriers

4.1 Bulk chemical carriers may be specialised to particular products or may have a number of tanks each of which may carry a different product. In any case, equipment for cargo carrying and handling, which may be complex, requires high standards of care in its maintenance and operation.

4.2 Guidance on general precautions which should be taken is given in the *Tanker Safety Guide* (*Chemicals*) and the booklet *Safety in Chemical Tankers*, both published by the International Chamber of Shipping. The IMCO recommended *Code for the Construction and Equipment of Ships Carrying Dangerous Liquid Chemicals in Bulk*, also contains guidance on operational needs. These publications should be available on board together with any special safety regulations issued by the company.

4.3 The appropriate provisions of section 2.4–2.10 and 3.5 should also be followed where applicable.

4.4 Where the cargo comprises or includes dangerous substances, the provisions of Chapter 27, section 2 apply.

4.5 Bulk chemical carriers often carry vegetable oils which require crew members to enter the tank and sweep the cargo to the tank suction and this often leads to cargo being brought up on to the deck on seaboots and clothing. This, added to the frequent sampling during loading and before discharge, causes the decks to become very slippery. Care should be taken to minimise the amount of cargo reaching the deck, but the dangers of slipping and falling should always be borne in mind when moving about the deck.

4.6 Many cargoes carried on this type of vessel are loosely referred to as alcohols. It should be emphasised that drinking these could lead to serious injury and death. Strict control should be exercised when carrying such cargoes in order to prevent pilferage.

4.7 Samples of chemical cargoes carried are often retained on board for long periods. These samples should be stowed in a special store and kept under lock and key. Where work is required to be carried out in these spaces, this should be closely monitored.

CHAPTER 30

Ferries, ro/ro carriers and car carriers

1 General

1.1 Seamen working on vehicle decks and in close proximity to moving vehicles should wear safety helmets and clothing of high visibility, such as fluorescent 'slip-overs'.

1.2 Suitable footwear should be worn to avoid risk of injury from securing gear.

1.3 Where no other means of access is provided, care should be taken by personnel using loading ramps for access while vehicles are moving on or off the ship.

1.4 Jacks, trestles and lashing equipment should not obstruct walkways, doorways or emergency escapes.

1.5 Ship's stores should not be stowed on any part of the parking area for vehicles.

1.6 A lifebuoy with self-activating light and line of suitable length should be available close to the vehicle deck access doors.

1.7 All decks should be kept free of water, oil and any other substance which might be conducive to a vehicle or cargo unit sliding.

1.8 Any spillage of petrol, oil or cargo should be cleaned up immediately; sand boxes, drip trays and equipment should be provided for such use on each vehicle deck.

1.9 There should be no smoking or use of naked lights on vehicle decks.

1.10 Notices setting out the precautions to be observed in handling and stowing vehicles should be prominently displayed in all vehicle spaces.

1.11 Any damage to electric lights and fittings should be repaired as soon as practicable.

1.12 A very high standard of crew fire drill is essential. A patrol should be maintained on vehicle decks during the passage.

2 Stowage of vehicles

2.1 All vehicles should be stowed in a fore and aft direction as far as practicable.

2.2 Any vehicle stowed athwartships should be securely lashed.

2.3 Vehicles should not be stowed across a water spray fire curtain.

2.4 Special care should be taken in positioning and securing a vehicle or cargo unit when decks are sparsely loaded to minimise the damage which would be caused by the vehicle breaking free into unrestricted space.

2.5 Vehicles containing dangerous cargoes should be handled in accordance with the *Code for portable tanks and road tank vehicles for the carriage of liquid dangerous goods in ships* or otherwise as directed in the 'Blue Book' and the *International Maritime Dangerous Goods Code* (IMDG Code). If tanks are found to be leaking or having evidence of possible leakage or otherwise significantly damaged so as to possibly affect the integrity of the tank, the vehicle should not be accepted for shipment. When the vehicle carries a transport emergency card (Tremcard) for its load, the card should be lodged with the Master for reference in case leaks should develop during the voyage.

2.6 Any vehicle carrying dangerous goods should be segregated from other cargo, accommodation, machinery openings and animals, in accordance with the 'Blue Book'. It should be readily accessible to an emergency party and, whenever practicable, located in a position convenient to fire-fighting services and drainage scuppers.

2.7 Personnel should not stand behind or between vehicles when these are manoeuvring.

2.8 Personnel should not attempt to secure a vehicle until the brakes have been applied and the engine switched off.

2.9 Lashing and securing of vehicles and cargo units should be carried out by men trained and experienced in the task.

2.10 There should be an adequate supply of efficient securing and lashing equipment which should be properly maintained and regularly inspected.

2.11 All lashings should have suitable tightening arrangements.

2.12 Lashings should be tightened to ensure that they are secure but not overtightened so that unnecessary strain is thrown upon the lashing. Care should be taken to equalise as far as practicable the tensions of the several lashings of a vehicle etc.

2.13 Personnel should not remain on internal deck ramps which are being raised or lowered.

3 Ventilation

3.1 Ventilation systems serving the vehicle decks should be in operation during loading and unloading and as may be necessary on passage to avoid the accumulation of flammable and toxic vapours.

3.2 Connecting doors between car-decks and machinery, service and accommodation spaces should be kept closed while the ship is at sea.

3.3 Conspicuous notices should be posted warning against the starting of vehicle engines before doors leading to ramps are opened and before the vehicle is required to move.

3.4 Any refrigerated vehicle needing to run its refrigeration plant during the voyage should utilise the ship's electrical supply where practicable, in preference to running its engine.

4 Portable car decks

4.1 Frequent inspections should be made of the equipment and associated gear used for raising, lowering and suspending portable decks.

4.2 Seamen should stand clear while portable decks are being raised or lowered. Should jamming occur, care should be taken in case of sudden release of the jam.

4.3 Portable stanchions and hand rails should always be in position when portable decks are in use.

4.4 Care should be taken to ensure that portable decks are properly stowed and secured when not in use.

4.5 When portable decks are in the stowed position, access doors should be secured.

CHAPTER 31

Ships serving offshore gas and oil installations

1 General

1.1 Ships serving offshore gas and oil installations often have to operate in adverse weather conditions. Work on deck in such conditions should be avoided if the movement of the ship would create special hazards.

1.2 The Master of the vessel has the final responsibility for ensuring that any operation is carried on with proper regard to the safety of all those on board and that measures are taken to minimise risks.

1.3 Where a vessel has open stern and deck gangway doors and a low freeboard, particular care should be taken against loss of watertight integrity by ensuring that scuttles, deadlights, hatches and ventilators are securely closed. Freeing ports should be kept clear and unobstructed to ensure the rapid drainage of water trapped on the deck.

1.4 While work is being done on deck, the vessel should be made as sea-kindly as practicable. A look-out should be posted to give warning of imminent oncoming, quartering or following seas.

1.5 At all times work is being done on deck, there should be an efficient means of communication between bridge and crew. This may be provided by the use of a portable 'talk-back' speaker which can be plugged into circuit points provided at working areas.

1.6 During hours of darkness, sufficient lighting should be provided at access ways and at any work location, to ensure that obstructions are clearly visible and that the operation may be carried out safely.

1.7 Lighting should be so placed that it does not dazzle the navigational watch and does not interfere with prescribed navigation lights.

1.8 During bad weather, lifelines should be rigged on the working deck to facilitate safe movement. Decks should as far as practicable be kept free from ice, slush and any substance or loose material likely to cause slips or falls.

1.9 Men working in cold and wet conditions should wear waterproof garments over warm clothing. The need to avoid undue exhaustion and hands and limbs becoming numbed should be taken into account when making the necessary arrangements for relief at suitable intervals.

1.10 Whenever there is a risk of falling, or being swept, overboard the seaman should wear some form of personal buoyancy of a type which would not unduly hamper or impede working movements. If it is necessary for a man to work in an exposed position he should, where practicable, wear a safety harness and lifeline.

1.11 Safety helmets should be worn during work on deck.

1.12 Advice on mooring and casting off is given in Chapter 16. Arrangements should be made to receive mooring lines, so as to avoid the necessity for seamen to jump ashore, a dangerous practice which has caused many accidents.

2 Carriage of cargo on deck

2.1 The safe securing of all deck cargoes should be checked by a competent person before the vessel proceeds on passage. To aid unloading at sea to be carried out safely, independent cargo units should, as far as practicable, be individually lashed. Lashings should, where practicable, be of a type that can be easily released and maintained (see also Chapter 27, section 1).

2.2 All lashings should be checked at least once during each watch whilst at sea. Personnel engaged in the operation should be closely supervised from the bridge, particularly in adverse weather conditions. At night in bad weather, an Aldis lamp or searchlight should be used to aid remote checking of lashings to avoid placing men at risk.

2.3 Discarded rope and damaged and unserviceable equipment and cargo should not be jettisoned at sea but retained for disposal ashore. Such materials and articles can foul propellers or cause damage to fishing gear.

3 Lifting, hauling and towing gear

3.1 All fixed and running gear should be carefully maintained in good order and regularly inspected to detect wear, damage and corrosion as recommended in Chapter 17. More frequent inspections should be made where gear has hard usage or is much exposed to sea and weather.

3.2 In all operations which may impose large loads or shock strains upon the gear, precautions should be taken against sudden failure which may cause injury to personnel. To the extent practicable, the system should be so designed that the weakest element is at a point where failure is likely to cause least danger.

3.3 While gear is under load, men essential for the operation should keep in protected positions to the greatest practicable extent. Others not engaged in the operations should keep clear of the working area.

4 Approaching rig and cargo handling at rig

4.1 Personnel should never stand forward of the windlass when letting go anchors at the rig. This is particularly important in vessels of this type because of the length of the chain and the loads thus imposed. Care should be taken when stowing the anchor cable in the locker (see Chapter 16).

4.2 In bad weather and under certain conditions of trim, considerable amounts of water may be shipped over the after-deck when the vessel is approaching a rig stern-on under power. Seamen should be alert to this possibility and seek positions of shelter and safety.

4.3 Care should be taken to keep clear when spring ropes are being lowered from the rig by crane.

4.4 Life-saving equipment, including lifebuoy, boathook and heaving line, should be readily available at a suitable position on the stern and other points of particular danger when mooring and while cargo handling is in progress.

4.5 In applying the recommendations of Chapter 17 to cargo handling, it should be borne in mind that transfer of cargo at sea is at any time a difficult operation and the risks are greatly increased when heavy or bulk items are being handled from a confined deck space in a seaway.

4.6 When cargo is being unloaded at the rig, the lashings of each individual item of cargo should not be released until the item is about to be lifted; there are grave risks if all cargo lashings are removed before unloading operations are begun.

4.7 Once unlashed prior to lifting, cargo should be secured against movement as much as possible by the use of large wooden wedges, sandbags or other effective means.

4.8 Personnel should be at all times alert to the danger of being hit or crushed should items of cargo swing during a lift or become dislodged through sudden movement of the ship. For this reason, all personnel should seek positions of safety as far as practicable during the lifting and lowering of cargo. If, in some circumstances, cargo hooks have to be held until the strain is taken, as when pipes are to be unloaded, crew members thus engaged should immediately move to a safe position before the actual lift is effected.

4.9 Lifts should be speedily effected to hoist the load well off the deck and swung clear of the ship as quickly as possible.

4.10 If any back-loading has to take place from the rig during off-loading of cargo from the vessel, care should be taken to ensure that the cargo taken on board is immediately secured against movement until it can be properly stowed.

4.11 It is essential that an efficient means of communication, preferably by radio link, is established between the rig crane operator and the working deck officer, who should at all times be in visual contact with each other.

5 Transfer of personnel from ship to rig by 'personnel baskets'

5.1 The following procedures should be observed for the transference of personnel from ship to rig by 'personnel baskets':

(a) two seamen should steady the equipment when it is lowered to the deck;

(b) luggage should be secured within the net of the basket;

(c) personnel to be transferred should wear lifejackets;

(d) personnel transferring should be evenly distributed around the base board to ensure maximum stability;

(e) personnel should stand outside the basket with feet apart on the board and the basket securely gripped with both arms looped through;

(f) when the officer in charge is satisfied that all is ready, and at an appropriate moment having regard to the movement of the ship in a seaway, the basket should be lifted clear of the vessel and then swung up and out as quickly as possible before being carefully hoisted up to the rig;

(g) throughout the operation, a lifebuoy, boathook and heaving line should be kept immediately available on board the vessel for use in case of emergencies;

6 Transfer of personnel by boat

6.1 The Master of the ship providing the boat should be responsible for the operation. Due consideration should be given to the effect of prevailing conditions on the safety of the transfer.

6.2 The boat should be reliably powered.

6.3 The boat should be crewed by not less than two experienced persons, at least one of whom should be experienced in handling the boat. Lifejackets and, if necessary, suitable protective clothing, should be worn by the crew and by the personnel carried.

6.4 A safety rope should be provided for all personnel ascending or descending overside by ship's ladder.

6.5 Boarding and disembarkation should be carried out in an orderly manner under the coxswain's direction.

6.6 The boat's coxswain should ensure an even and safe distribution of passengers. Passengers should not stand up or change their positions during the passage between ships save under instructions from the coxswain.

6.7 The parent vessel should establish communication with the receiving vessel prior to the commencement of the operation and should maintain continuous visual contact with the boat concerned throughout the transfer. It is recommended that the boat should carry a VHF radio.

6.8 If the transfer of personnel involves a stand-by vessel, the Master should bear in mind that his vessel must at all times be ready to fulfill its stand-by vessel duties.

7 Anchor handling

7.1 Handling rig anchors at sea can be a particularly hazardous and arduous task. The vessel should be controlled in such a manner to minimise the risks concerned, in particular, to avoid as far as possible an anchor wire under heavy load whipping from quarter to quarter across the deck.

7.2 The provisions of section 3.3 on the need for crew members to keep to protected positions are particularly important during the handling of anchors and anchor buoys.

7.3 Anchor buoys being lifted aboard should be kept clear of the working area and lashed immediately upon landing to prevent movement.

7.4 Care should be taken when stoppering off wires.

7.5 When anchors are let go over the stern, all personnel should be well forward of the stern and in protected positions.

APPENDIX 1

Standards

The British Standard Specifications extant at 31 December 1977 which are relevant to recommendations in the Code are listed below. Work on revising and developing standards proceeds continuously and, where it is found that a listed standard has been superseded, the most up-to-date version should be adopted. Generally, a British Standard closely corresponds with an International Standard where one exists, and the references of corresponding ISO (International Standards Organisation) standards are given for guidance where equipment has to be obtained in foreign ports.

CHAPTER 1 General

3 Working clothes

BS 5426: 1976 *Specifications for work wear*

CHAPTER 5 Protective clothing and equipment

1 Head protection

BS 4033: 1966 *Industrial scalp protectors (light duty)*
BS 5240: 1975 *General purpose industrial safety helmets*

2 Eye protection

BS 2092: 1967 *Industrial eye protectors*

3 Respiratory protective equipment

BS 4275: 1974 *Recommendations for the selection, use and maintenance of respiratory protective equipment*

(a) *Respirators*

BS 2091: 1969 *Respirators for protection against harmful dust, gases and scheduled agricultural chemicals*
BS 4555: 1970 *High efficiency dust respirators*
BS 4558: 1970 *Positive pressure, powered dust respirators*

(b) *Breathing apparatus*

BS 4667: Part 1: 1974 *Closed-circuit breathing apparatus*
BS 4667: Part 2: 1974 *Open-circuit breathing apparatus*
BS 4667: Part 3: 1974 *Fresh air hose and compressed air line breathing apparatus*

BS 4667: Part 4: 1975 *Escape breathing apparatus*

4 Gloves

BS 1651: 1966 *Industrial gloves*

BS 697: 1960 *Rubber gloves for electrical purposes* (see Chapters 22 and 23)

5 Footwear

BS 1870: Part 1: 1970 *Safety boots and shoes other than all-rubber types*

BS 1870: Part 2: 1976 *Lined rubber safety boots*

6 Safety belts and harnesses

BS 1397: 1967 *Industrial safety belts and harnesses*

7 Rubber mats (see Chapters 22 and 23)

BS 921: 1976 *Rubber mats for electrical purposes*

CHAPTER 6 Signs, notices and colour codes

1 Safety signs, colour codes

BS 5378: 1976 *Safety colours and safety signs* (partially agrees with ISO/DIS 3864)

2 Fire extinguishers

BS 5423: 1971 *Portable fire extinguishers*

3 Gas cylinders

BS 349: 1973 *Identification of contents of industrial gas containers* (incorporates ISO/R 448)

BS 1319: 1976 *Medical gas cylinders, valves and yoke connections* (agrees with ISO/R 32 and ISO/R 407)

4 Pipelines

BS 1710: 1975 *Identification of pipelines* (substantially agrees with ISO/R 508)

CHAPTER 8 Accommodation ladders, gangways and other means of access

BS MA 78: 1977 *Shipbuilding specification of aluminium shore gangways*

BS 3913: 1973 *Industrial safety nets*

SIS 7 (Shipbuilding Industry Standard) *Weatherdeck ladders (bulwark)*

CHAPTER 9 Movement about the ship

BS MA 40: Part 20: 1975 (Marine Series) *Gates and portable guardrail sections for merchant ships (excluding passenger ships)*

CHAPTER 12 Tools and materials
BS 6500: 1975 *Insulated flexible cords* (partially agrees with IEC 227 and 245)

CHAPTER 13 Welding and flamecutting
BS 638: 1966 *Arc welding plant, equipment and accessories*
BS 697: 1959 *Filters for use during welding and similar industrial operations*
BS 1542: 1960 *Equipment for eye, face and neck protection against radiation arising during welding and similar operations*
BS 2653: 1955 *Protective clothing for welders*

CHAPTERS 15 and 16 Ropes
BS 365: 1968 *Galvanised steel wire ropes for ships*
BS 2052: 1965 *Ropes made from coir, hemp, manila and sisal*
BS 4128: 1967 *Recommendations for the selection, use and care of man-made ropes in marine applications*
BS 4928: Part 1: 1973 *Polypropylene ropes 13-strand hawser laid and 8-strand plaited* (agrees with ISO/R 1346)
BS 4928: Part 2: 1974 *Polyamide (nylon), polyester and polyethylene filament ropes* (agrees with ISO/R 1140, R 1141 and R 1969)
SIS 23 (Shipbuilding Industry Standard) *Stoppers for mooring ropes*

CHAPTER 18 Hatches
BS 4263: 1967 *Marking of hatchway beams* (based on ISO/R 151)
BS 4268: 1967 *Marking of wooden hatchway covers* (based on ISO/R 152)

APPENDIX 2

Bibliography

1 HMSO publications
(available from HMSO bookshops and agents, or if asterisked * direct from the Enquiry Point, Health and Safety Executive, Baynards House, 1–13 Chepstow Place, London W2 4TF)

(a) Health and Safety at Work Booklets
No 4 *Safety in the Use of Abrasive Wheels*
No 18 *Industrial Dermatitis – Precautionary Measures*
No 19 *Safety in Laundries*
No 20 *Drilling Machines – Guarding of Spindles and Attachments*
No 25 *Noise and the Worker*
No 31 *Safety in Electrical Testing*
No 35 *Basic Rules for Safety and Health at Work*
No 44 *Asbestos: Health Precautions in Industry*
No 50 *Welding and Flame-cutting using Compressed Gases*

(b) Advisory Publications
(i) Safety and Health at Work Leaflets
SHW 25* *Safe use of ladders*
SHW 264* *Abrasive Wheels – Safety in Installation and Use*
(ii) Advisory Leaflets
IAL1* *Fires and Explosions due to the misuse of oxygen*
MS(A)3* *Asbestos and you*
(iii) Cautionary Cards
MS(B)3* *Anthrax*
MS(B)6* *Occupational (Industrial) Dermatitis*

(c) Guidance Notes from the Health & Safety Executive
(i) General Series
GS 1 *Fumigation using methyl bromide (bromomethane)*
GS 5 *Entry into confined spaces*
(ii) Chemical Series
CS 1 *Industrial use of flammable gas detectors*

(iii) Environmental Hygiene Series
EH 13 *Beryllium – health and safety precautions*
EH 15 *Threshold limit values for 1976*
(iv) Medical Series
MS 2 *Anthrax*
MS 7 *Colour vision*

(d) Certificates of Approval
F2486 Certificate of Approval (Respiratory Protective Equipment) 1977

(e) *Carriage of Dangerous Goods in Ships* – Report of the Standing Advisory Committee (the 'Blue Book')

(f) Department of Trade *Code of Practice on Noise Levels in Ships*

(g) *Ship Captain's Medical Guide*

2 International Chamber of Shipping (ICS) Publications
(produced by the International Chamber of Shipping, 30/32 St Mary Axe, London EC3A 8ET)
International Safety Guide for Oil Tankers and Terminals
Tanker Safety Guide (Chemicals)
Tanker Safety Guide (Liquefied Gas)
Safety in Oil Tankers (handbook for crew members)
Safety in Chemical Tankers (handbook for crew members)
Guide to Helicopter/Tanker Operations

3 Other Publications
International Maritime Dangerous Goods Code (IMDG Code), (published by the Intergovernmental Maritime Consultative Organization (IMCO), 101 Piccadilly, London W1)
IMDG Medical Guide (published by IMCO as above)
Reference Book of Protective Equipment (published by the Industrial Safety (Protective Equipment) Manufacturers Association, 69 Cannon Street, London EC4)
Code of Practice for the Safe Carriage of Dangerous Goods in Freight Containers (published by the General Council of British Shipping, 30/32 St Mary Axe, London EC3A 8ET)
Accident prevention on board ship at sea and in port (Code of Practice) (published by the International Labour Office (ILO), Geneva and available from the ILO London office, 87 New Bond Street, London W1)

Index

References are to chapter paragraph numbers, not page numbers.

References are to chapter paragraph numbers, not page numbers.

References are to chapter paragraph numbers, not page numbers.

References are to chapter paragraph numbers, not page numbers.

References are to chapter paragraph numbers, not page numbers.

References are to chapter paragraph numbers, not page numbers.

References are to chapter paragraph numbers, not page numbers.

References are to chapter paragraph numbers, not page numbers.

References are to chapter paragraph numbers, not page numbers.

References are to chapter paragraph numbers, not page numbers.

References are to chapter paragraph numbers, not page numbers.

References are to chapter paragraph numbers, not page numbers.

References are to chapter paragraph numbers, not page numbers.

Printed for Her Majesty's Stationery Office
by Hobbs the Printers of Southampton
(1131) Dd718998 C75 6/81 G3927